Vatic
Facing the 21st Century

Historical and
Theological Perspectives

EDITED BY
DERMOT A. LANE AND BRENDAN LEAHY

VERITAS

Published 2006 by
Veritas Publications
7/8 Lower Abbey Street
Dublin 1
Ireland
Email publications@veritas.ie
Website www.veritas.ie

10 9 8 7 6 5 4 3 2 1

ISBN 1 84730 012 X
978 1 84730 012 6 (from January 2007)

Scripture quotes from *The New Revised Standard Version Bible: Catholic
Edition* © 1993 and 1998 by the Division of Christian Education of the
National Council of the Churches of Christ in the United States of America.
Extract from John McGahern's *Memoir* courtesy of Faber and Faber Limited
(p. 146).

A catalogue record for this book is available from the British Library.

Designed by Colette Dower
Printed in the Republic of Ireland by Betaprint, Dublin

*Veritas books are printed on paper made from the wood pulp of
managed forests. For every tree felled, at least one tree is planted,
thereby renewing natural resources.*

Contents

Contributors   5

Introduction   9

1.   An Eyewitness Account   13
     Bishop Michael Smith

2.   *Gaudium et spes:*
     The Church in the Modern World   31
     Most Rev. Diarmuid Martin

3.   People, Synod and Upper Room:
     Vatican II's Ecclesiology of Communion   49
     Brendan Leahy

4.   The Cornerstones of Liturgical Renewal:
     Sacrosanctum concilium   81
     Susan K. Roll

5.   *Dei verbum* Forty Years Later   99
     Jan Lambrecht SJ

6.   A Renewed Theology of Divine Revelation:
     Response to Jan Lambrecht   130
        Thomas Norris

7.   The Relationship between the
     Old Testament and the New Testament
     according to *Dei verbum*   136
        Beate Kowalski

8.   Religious Education since Vatican II:
     Significant Voices   146
        Maura Hyland

9.   Ecumenism Forty Years on –
     Are we Still in the Desert?   187
        M. Cecily Boulding OP

10. *Nostra aetate*: Encountering other Religions,
     Enriching the Theological Imagination   202
        Dermot A. Lane

Index   237

Contributors

Cecily Boulding OP is a former lecturer in theology at Ushaw College, the University of Durham and Oscott College. From 1983–1991 she was a member of the Anglican–Roman Catholic International Commission (ARCIC) and from 1988–2001 the Catholic Bishops of England and Wales' representative on the Formal Conversations between Anglicans and Methodists. She is the author of *The Church in Ecumenical Perspective* (2001).

Maura Hyland has been working in religious education in Ireland since the 1970s as a teacher, catechist and author of religious education texts for use at the national level. She is currently Director of Veritas Communications, an agency of the Irish Catholic Bishops' Conference and Publisher of the National Catechetical Programmes of Ireland.

Beate Kowalski holds the Terence Albert O'Brien Chair of Biblical Studies at the Department of Theology and Religious Studies, Mary Immaculate College, University of Limerick. Her theological doctorate dissertation in

Ruhr-Univeristaet Bochum/Germany was on the Good Shepherd Discourse in John 10:1-18 (published in 1996). Her *Habilitation* in the Leopold-Franzens-Universitaet Innsbruck/Austria was on the Reception of the Prophet Ezekiel in Revelation of John (published in 2004).

Jan Lambrecht SJ is Professor Emeritus of New Testament and Biblical Greek at the Catholic University of Leuven. He has also taught the New Testament at the Pontifical Biblical Institute in Rome. He was a member of the Pontifical Biblical Commission from 1985 to 1995. Among his recent publications are *Understanding What One Reads: New Testament Essays* (2003), *Collected Studies on Pauline Literature and on the Book of Revelation* (2001) and *Second Corinthians* (1999).

Dermot A. Lane is President of Mater Dei Institute of Education and Parish Priest of Balally in south Dublin. He is the author of numerous works including *The Experience of God: An Invitation to do Theology*, revised and expanded edition, 2003, and editor of *Catholic Theology Facing the Future: Historical Perspectives*, 2003.

Brendan Leahy, formerly Registar of Mater Dei Institute of Education, is currently Professor of Systematic Theology at St Patrick's College, Maynooth. He is secretary to the Bishops' Conference Advisory Committee on Ecumenism, author of *The Marian Profile in the Ecclesiology of Hans Urs von Balthasar* (2000) and co-author with Thomas Norris of *Christianity: its Origins and Contemporary Expressions* (2003).

Diarmuid Martin is Archbishop of Dublin, Primate of Ireland and formerly the Holy See Permanent Observer in

Geneva at the United Nations Office and at the World Trade Organisation. He has represented the Holy See at major United Nations International Conferences and has lectured extensively on the Church's Social Doctrine and Vatican II's vision of the Church in the modern world.

Thomas Norris is a lecturer in systematic theology at St Patrick's College, Maynooth. A member of the International Theological Commission since 1998, he has written extensively on the thought and writings of Cardinal John Henry Newman. He is author of *Only Life gives Life: Revelation, Theology and Christian Living according to Cardinal Newman* (1996) and *Thinking about Education* (forthcoming).

Susan K. Roll is Associate Professor of Theology, specialising in Liturgy and Sacraments, in the Faculty of Theology at St Paul University, Ottawa, Canada, and the Director of the Centre for Women and Christian Traditions at the University. She has published numerous articles and is author of *Towards the Origins of Christmas* (1995).

Michael Smith is Bishop of the diocese of Meath and member of the Department of Planning and Communications of the Irish Bishops' Conference. He witnessed the Second Vatican Council first hand as he was one of the group that was entrusted with the task of compiling the official record or *Acta* of the Council.

Introduction

The Second Vatican Council (1962–1965) stands out as one of the most influential events in the history of the Catholic Church and certainly the most important event of the twentieth century for Catholicism. Vatican II is also of special significance to Mater Dei Institute of Education because it was founded by John Charles McQuaid, Archbishop of Dublin, in 1966 – one year after the closure of the council. Clearly the Institute is a child of the Council in conception, identity and mission. The purpose of the foundation of Mater Dei Institute was to provide teachers for second-level schools in Ireland who had a specialist qualification in Religious Education. Given this background it was important for the Institute to mark in some small way the fortieth anniversary of the closure of the Second Vatican Council.

The reception of the Council has been a matter of considerable debate within the Church. When it came to the celebration of the twentieth anniversary of the conclusion of the Council in 1985, the Extraordinary Synod of Bishops meeting in Rome drew up guidelines for the interpretation of the Council. These guidelines included the following points:

1. The theological interpretation of the conciliar doctrine must consider all the documents, both in themselves and in their close inter-relationship, so that the integral meaning of the Council's affirmations – often very complex – might be understood and expressed;
2. Special attention must be paid to the four major Constitutions of the Council, which are the keys to the interpretation of other Decrees and Declarations;
3. It is not licit to separate the pastoral character from the doctrinal force of the documents;
4. No opposition may be made between the spirit and the letter of the Council;
5. The Council must be understood in continuity with the great tradition of the Church and, at the same time, we must receive light from the Council's own doctrine for today's Church and the men of our time (1985 Synod, 'The Final Report', Part 1, section 5).

The historical reception and theological interpretation of the teaching of the Council continues to be a matter of lively discussion within the life of the Church. Thus it was hardly surprising that when Pope Benedict XVI came to comment on the fortieth anniversary of the closure of the Council in his message to the Curia on 22 December 2005 he discussed the issue of the proper interpretation of the Council. He noted that two different and contrary hermeneutics have come face to face in their understanding and interpretation of the Council. The first mode of interpretation he refers to as 'the hermeneutic of discontinuity and rupture'. This particular approach 'risks ending in a split between the pre-Conciliar Church and the post-Conciliar Church'. Further, this approach holds that the texts of the Council do not express the true spirit of the Council. The second approach he calls the 'hermeneutic of reform', which is reflected in the speech of Pope John XXIII inaugurating the Council on 11 October 1962 and the closing speech of Paul VI on 7 December 1965. According to Benedict XVI, true reform consists in a 'combination of continuity and discontinuity at different levels' (address to the Curia on 22 December 2005).

It was in this context of the historical reception and theological interpretation of the Council that Mater Dei decided to host a series of Public Lectures on 'Vatican II – Forty Years On' in the autumn of 2005. The purpose of this series of lectures was to celebrate the fortieth anniversary of the closure of the Council, and at the same time try to communicate the content of some of the documents. It was not the intention of the Institute to address all of the documents. Instead, following the guidelines of the 1985 Synod, it decided to focus on the four main Constitutions as the hermeneutical key for approaching the other documents of the Council. The four Constitutions are:

- Constitution on the Sacred Liturgy (4 December 1963);
- Dogmatic Constitution on the Church (21 November 1964);
- Dogmatic Constitution on Divine Revelation (18 November 1965);
- Pastoral Constitution on the Church in the Modern World (7 December 1965).

In addition to and in the context of the four Constitutions, the Institute also decided to address two particular documents that have a direct bearing on the identity of the Institute as a College of Education specialising in Religious Education. Of key importance to the life of the Institute is the *Decree on Ecumenism* (21 November 1964) and the challenges it poses for Religious Education today. Also of great significance for the Institute is the increasingly important *Declaration on the Relationship of the Church to the Non-Christian Religions* (28 October 1965) and the growing importance of inter-religious dialogue within Religious Education.

Also central to the Institute is the discipline of Religious Education. Thus, a special lecture is devoted to developments in Religious Education in the light of Vatican II.

In addition to the four Constitutions, these two specialised documents on ecumenism and inter-religious dialogue, and the discipline of Religious Education, it was also necessary to have a sense of the historical context of the Council and so an opening lecture was given over to locating Vatican II within the history of the twentieth century.

The purview of these published papers on the Council, therefore, does not pretend in any way to be comprehensive. Instead, the focus is quite limited: limited to the four major Constitutions as key to any understanding of the Council, to what the Council had to say specifically on Ecumenism and Inter-Religious Dialogue as central to the mission of Mater Dei Institute, to an overview of Religious Education in the light of the Council and to a historical introduction to the Council. The selection of documents, therefore, has been influenced by the identity of the Institute as a Catholic College of Education specialising in Religious Education. It is hoped that the publication of these papers will renew interest in the vision of the Second Vatican Council and its ongoing relevance to some of the educational challenges facing the Catholic Church in the twenty-first century in Ireland.

Dermot A. Lane and Brendan Leahy
Mater Dei Institute of Education
Dublin City University
Clonliffe Road, Dublin 3
1 March 2006

An Eyewitness Account

Bishop Michael Smith

I welcome this series of lectures being organised by Mater Dei Institute forty years after the end of the Second Vatican Council. I am honoured to be invited to begin the series with a personal recollection of that pivotal event in the life of the Church. Obviously one lecture could not even begin to touch on all aspects of the Council so I will confine myself to some of its key moments, as well as reflecting on the events which led up to the holding of the Council. In these I believe Divine Providence was very clearly at work. I certainly do not belong to those who feel that the Council was a mistake or even, as some have claimed, a disaster for the Church.

I will begin by explaining how I can come here this evening sharing my personal recollections of the Council. Towards the end of 1961 the Rector of the Irish College asked if I would be willing to become involved in the group that was to be entrusted with the task of compiling the official record or *Acta* of the Council. This would involve learning Latin shorthand. I was then in my third theology year at the college studying at the Lateran University and obviously I didn't need to be asked twice. In all, forty-two students drawn from the seminaries in Rome were invited to take part, the majority of them Italian. We had a German teacher who had devised his own system of Latin shorthand, Dr Aloys Kennernecht.

As well as following our normal course in the university we also attended classes most evenings at the Vatican. It was an interesting if demanding experience. In the end the group became twelve and with one or two changes this small group was present for all four years of the Council. While we did not have to attend every day, most of us did. Apart from the opportunity to take part in such a major event (only twenty councils had taken place in the previous 2,000 years) it was also a formative experience and an education not to be missed. My memory of that involvement is still very fresh and while it made extra demands on theological and post-graduate studies I have no regrets giving it that time.

The first comment I would wish to share with you is my own strong belief that Divine Providence was deeply involved in the life of Bl. John XXIII and his project to hold a Council. This was manifested over many decades but it is only in hindsight that we can see with greater clarity the hand of God at work.

The Context and Background
On 25 January 1959 in St Paul's Outside the Wall Pope John XXIII's announcement of his intention to call a General Council of the Church took everyone by surprise. At the same time, he announced his intention to hold a Synod of the Diocese of Rome and to prepare a new edition of the Code of Canon Law. Since then it has been accepted that the reaction of the cardinals present on that occasion was somewhat less than enthusiastic. This has been portrayed as an indication of their unhappiness with the

Pope's decision. However, there is another side to the story. Seldom has their reaction been placed in its proper context.

The First Vatican Council came to a hurried end with Garibaldi's army at the gates of Rome. The Council, with the strong encouragement of Bl. Pius IX, decided to give precedence to the decree on Papal Infallibility and complete it, leaving the other matters on the agenda for consideration at a later date. The assumption was that when things settled down again the Council could resume. This proved impossible in the immediate aftermath of the Council, given the political climate in the newly unified Italian State.

Although the intention to resume the Council was not forgotten, Leo XIII, St Pius X and Benedict XV do not seem to have taken any action to fulfil this wish, whatever their desire might have been. Shortly after his election in 1922 Pius XI presided over the International Eucharistic Congress held in Rome at which over three hundred bishops were present. This prompted him to consider reconvening Vatican I. In December of 1922 he stated in an encyclical letter his wish to finish the Council begun by Bl. Pius IX. His intention was to convene the bishops of the Church in Rome in the Holy Year 1925. His first challenge was to find where the archives of the Council were stored. When eventually the room was identified the difficulty was then to find the key! When the room was opened the archives were found to be in a poor and disorganised state. He first had them catalogued and then set up a small group of four theologians to examine them in detail and come up with proposals.

The experts, while leaning heavily in the direction of a Council condemning doctrinal errors, did propose that a reflection on the Church should be its primary focus. They also highlighted the need for an examination of the role of women in the Church and in society. In October 1923 all the bishops of the Church were consulted by letter on the appropriateness of reconvening the Council. Eighty per cent of the 1,165 cardinals and bishops canvassed replied by the deadline. The Pope personally read all the replies: well over half – 657 – agreed; 256 agreed, but with reservations; only 34 gave a negative response. Inevitably progress was slow and the target date of 1925 soon vanished. The large crowds that came to Rome for the Holy Year in 1925 also diverted attention from the proposal. At the end of the year Pius XI decided that priority should be given to finding a solution to the 'Roman Question' – the relationship between the Holy See and Italy. While this issue was resolved in 1929 the rapidly changing political scene in Europe precluded further consideration of the proposal to reconvene Vatican I and the Pope did not return to the issue.

The proposal resurfaced during the pontificate of Pius XII. Following a suggestion by Cardinal Ruffini to call a Council, Pius XII discussed the proposal with Cardinal Ottaviani, then Assessor at the Holy Office, in February 1948. Cardinal Ottaviani, who was to have a major role in preparing Vatican II, outlined many of the doctrinal and pastoral issues that merited consideration and gave the proposal qualified support. A fortnight later Cardinal Ottaviani gathered a group to discuss in detail the proposal to call a Council. It would seem from the records available that they were thinking at this stage of a new Council and not a reconvening of the unfinished Vatican I.

For two years considerable work was done in preparation for a Council. Reflecting the climate of the time the emphasis was on doctrinal integrity, condemnation of error and on discipline in the Church. In 1949 Pius XII appointed a Central Preparatory Committee with a President and Secretary, some of whom – notably Fr Bea, later cardinal – were to play a prominent role in Vatican II.

It is interesting that as secretary Pius XII chose Fr Peter Charles SJ, professor of dogmatic theology at Louvain: Louvain professors were to have a profound influence on Vatican II.

A letter to be sent out to sixty-five selected bishops was drafted and redrafted many times but does not seem to have been sent. Again the emphasis in this letter, discussed at several meetings of the Preparatory Committee, leaned strongly towards discipline and condemnation of error. One good example of how detailed the discussion was is provided by the proposals on the age for ordination to the priesthood. It was proposed to fix the age for receiving sub-diaconate at twenty-four, followed by a two-year probationary period before diaconate, followed by another year before priesthood. Sub-diaconate, it was proposed, would not be received until theological studies were complete.

As the work continued divisions arose between those proposing a short Council and those seeking the discussion of the many major challenges facing the Church, especially in the aftermath of the war and the impact of the 'Iron Curtain'. There was also a major difference of emphasis between the proposals prepared by the theological and the scriptural committees. Another division centred on what focus the Council should have – a doctrinal or a pastoral Council. The divisions were deep and could not be resolved by the Preparatory Committee.

In January 1951 the Committee decided to pass the problem to the Pope for resolution. The major illness he suffered shortly afterwards as well as other considerations meant that he never made a final decision and the matter was shelved. A number of the proposals that emerged in the preparatory work, primarily from the doctrinal committee, did find their way into documents and decisions made by Pius XII in following years, one example being the changes in the law on fasting before the reception of Holy Communion.

Many of the cardinals and others who heard Bl. John XXIII state that he was going to call an Ecumenical Council of the Church had invested a great amount of time and energy in preparing for a Council under Pius XII. They could be forgiven for thinking 'Not again!' A few, notably Cardinal Confalonieri who had been secretary to Pius XI, were also involved in the effort made in the early 1920s. It was Cardinal Confalonieri who presided at the funeral Mass for Pope John Paul I.

While Bl. John XXIII would have been aware of the work carried out in the early 1920s in response to Pius XI's initiative, statements made by people who were very close to him suggest that when he made his announcement he was unaware of the more detailed work carried out some years previously under Pius XII. His own version was that the idea came to him in prayer and he shared it with Cardinal Tardini, who warmly welcomed the proposal. He discussed it with very few, obviously deciding it was best to make his decision public and then deal with the problems and issues that would arise.

Had the initiative of Pius XI or that of Pius XII come to fruition it would have been a very different Council. Pope John did not share the outlook or understanding they brought to their own conciliar project. It was to be pastoral and ecumenical, it was to reach out to the world rather than adopt a defensive posture, it was to be short on condemnation and strong on proclaiming the fullness of the Gospel. With hindsight it is easy to see the hand of the Lord at work in his life, preparing him to launch this initiative on an unsuspecting Church. His opening address to the Council, which repays reading forty-three years later, only serves to emphasise how deeply Divine Providence was at work in his life.

The Council Hall and the Irish Contribution

The preparation for the Council brought out the best in Italian flair and genius. While the many commissions worked away at preparing the draft documents, others had to deal with the enormous logistical demands involved. As so often happens on such occasions gifted people surfaced. One such was Dr Francesco Vacchini, who designed the Council Hall in St Peter's, giving each bishop his own seat with a writing desk (over 2,500 in all) and making provision for all the ancillary services, including our small group. It worked like a dream with perfect acoustics and no real hitches over the four years. I was in the Hall about a week before the opening of the Council and one wondered how it could possibly be ready in time. On the day all was in place.

The appointment of Archbishop Felici was an inspired choice. He was a person of strong personality but also of great competence. He was a gifted Latin scholar who occasionally, when making the announcements at the start of each working day, recited one of his newly composed Latin poems, in the process testing our limited skill in Latin shorthand.

In all there were four periods of the Council with 168 sessions over the years 1962 to 1965, each held in the autumn and lasting around two months. In truth one could say there were three periods with one preparatory period. Given the very large number involved it was inevitable that it would take time for the Council to find its feet. Pope John wisely kept rules for procedure to the minimum and major adjustments were made between the first and second period. If the new rules of procedure, adopted after the experience of the first session, had been imposed from the beginning, especially that governing the closure of debate on individual topics, the Roman Curia would have been accused of trying to stifle debate. Pope John had learned well from his studies of previous Councils.

Overall the Irish contribution to the Council was disappointing. The submissions sent in by the individual bishops were largely in the area of law and discipline and there is no record in the minutes of the Bishops' Conference, from the date of its announcement to its opening, of the Council being discussed at meetings. The contribution made by the bishops during the first period of the Council to the debates makes this clear. Two short speeches (one lasting two minutes and the other five) were made by Archbishop McQuaid of Dublin in the name of all the bishops (Cardinal Dalton was then ill and died shortly after the end of this first period). These were made during the debate on the Liturgy. Neither made an impact on the final text.

Bishop Philbin did, however, make his own valuable contributions during the course of the Council, as did Cardinal Conway when he succeeded Cardinal Dalton. I will return to one of Bishop Philbin's contributions later. One disappointing feature of the Irish contribution was that little effort was made by the bishops to inform the people about what was taking place. They perhaps took more seriously than others the secrecy attaching to the discussions in the Council Hall. The same was true of the minimal support given to the Irish media representatives present in Rome. One national newspaper sent out a very senior staff member. Towards the end of the first period he commented that he considered his efforts over the two months as his biggest failure as a journalist. It was an opportunity lost.

Secrecy in fact went out the window from the beginning of the second session. The office looking after the interests of the American bishops decided to print in English a daily summary of all the talks given in the Council Hall that day. Since the texts of the talks were in our office a few of us along with a number of American *periti* (experts in theology, scripture, canon law etc.) became involved in this exercise. This 'Council Digest' as it was called was made available that same evening to any English-speaking bishops that requested it. By the time the fourth session came around over 2,000 copies were made available each day to bishops from every country.

What I have said up to now is seeking to place the Council in its context. Pope John had learned wisely from history and he was clear in his own mind that once the bishops were in Rome the Council would over time find its feet. He had no fear that it would go astray, as he had a deeply held belief in the guidance of the Holy Spirit. He even remarked on one occasion that he expected differences and difficulties to arise but was confident that in the end all would be fine.

During his time in the diplomatic service he was left for many years in Bulgaria and Turkey, neither demanding posts. It was during this time that he involved himself in a study of the Council of Trent and its implementation in the dioceses in Northern Italy, especially his own native diocese of Bergamo. He was very familiar with the previous Councils of the Church and knew that his Council would echo previous experience. A good example is found in what happened to the preparatory work. In total, over seventy documents were prepared for debate and discussion. Between the end of the first session and the beginning of the second these were reduced to less that twenty, reflecting the clear wishes of the Council. The same happened to the documents prepared for the First Vatican Council.

A Few of the Key Days

It would be impossible in a short talk to do justice to what was a major event in the life of the Church, an event that will influence the mission of the Church over centuries. I will just mention a few of the key days that gave the Council direction and focus.

The most important of all these was the opening day and especially the homily preached by Pope John on that occasion. It is worth quoting some of it:

> In the daily exercise of our pastoral office, we sometimes have to listen, much to our regret, to voices of persons who, though burning with zeal, are not endowed with too much sense of discretion or balance. In these modern times they can see nothing but prevarication and ruin. They say that our era, in comparison with past eras, is getting worse, and they behave as though they had learned nothing from history, which is, none the less, the teacher of life. They behave as though at the time of former Councils everything was a full triumph for the Christian idea and life and for proper religious liberty. We feel we must disagree with those prophets of gloom, who are always forecasting disaster, as though the end of the world was at hand. In the present order of things, Divine Providence is leading us to a new order of human relations which, by men's own efforts and even beyond their very expectations, are directed toward the fulfilment of God's superior and inscrutable designs. And everything, even human differences, leads to the greater good of the Church.

It is a passage that underlines Pope John's deep trust in Divine Providence, displays a clear understanding of history and seeks to place the Council in that historical context. He was also making clear that he was not for turning. The homily had an enormous impact on all who had gathered for the Council as it set out clearly what was expected of them. It would be fair to say that its content surprised many of the bishops.

Each day began with Mass and the enthronement of the Book of the Gospels. Pope John had appointed ten Presidents who took it in turn to preside over the daily sessions. They were not very effective and in a classical Italian move before the start of the second period Pope Paul increased their number to twelve and took most of their power away, handing over the daily chairing of the sessions to four moderators. However, two of the presidents did use their position on the first day of business to place a proposal before the bishops. Cardinal Frings of Cologne and Cardinal Lienart of Lille both suggested that the Council not meet for a few days to allow bishops to get to know one another. The agenda for that day had included voting for the membership of the Commissions that would have responsibility for the drafting of the decrees of the Council. Their proposal was accepted and that first day turned out to be the shortest working day of the Council. The few days of lobbying and consultation that followed undoubtedly had a major impact on the membership of the Commissions and, through them, on the documents that emanated from the Council.

Another day that had a major influence on the future direction of the Council was the 14 November – the beginning of the debate on the document on Scripture and Tradition. The debate on this document was led by eleven cardinals and one patriarch (cardinals had precedence when it came to speaking). The customary rush at mid-morning to the two coffee bars in St Peter's was absent that day.

Only one of the speakers defended the text and one gave it qualified support. The rest were trenchant in their criticism. The document was discussed over five days and the tone did not change. A vote was taken: 1,368 voted against the text, 822 voted in favour and there 19 spoiled votes. A two-thirds majority was needed to replace a text and it was announced that the debate would continue. However, Pope John intervened and appointed a special commission to prepare a new text. There were two Irish scripture scholars involved in this exercise, Cardinal Michael Browne OP, and Fr Alexander Kerrigan, an Irish Franciscan who spent his life in Rome, lecturing in scripture and working in the Curia.

The debate on this text also gave rise to another important intervention. This was made by Bishop de Smedt of Belgium in the name of the Secretariat of Christian Unity, headed by the highly respected Jesuit, Cardinal Bea. This set out the ecumenical guidelines that had to be respected in formulating all Council documents. It was greeted by warm applause and few doubted that the content of this intervention had been cleared with Pope John before it was delivered in the Council Hall.

An even more important intervention was that of Cardinal Suenens of Brussels on 3 December 1962. The debate had already begun on the document on the Church. Cardinal Suenens proposed that there was a need for two documents, one a reflection on the Church *ad intra* and the other *ad extra* if the Council was to be faithful to the mandate given it by Pope John. It later emerged that this intervention was prepared in consultation with Cardinal Montini, later Pope Paul VI, and Pope John. Cardinal Montini had kept a very low profile during this first session, gossip suggesting this was on the instructions of Pope John. He worked very closely with the Pope during this period and there is little doubt that Pope John would have seen him as his obvious successor and the one who would bring the Council to completion. Though different in personality they were very close in spirit and shared the same vision.

At the end of the session it was decided to take up this proposal, the outcome of which produced the two foundation documents on the Council: one on the Church (*Lumen gentium*) and the other on the Church in the Modern World (*Gaudium et spes*). Providence was at work here as well, as one of those who became deeply involved in the preparation of the document on the Church in the Modern World was the young Archbishop of Cracow, Archbishop Wojtyla. Another who worked on this document was Father (later cardinal) Yves Congar, the French Dominican theologian. In his Journal of the Council, Fr Congar made this interesting observation of Archbishop Woytyla in February 1965: 'Woytyla makes a big impression. His personality imposes itself. It shines forth with a mysterious power, an attraction, a certain prophetic power that is very calm but indisputable'. The content of this document on the Church in the Modern World was the quarry from which Pope John Paul drew so much of his teaching as Pope.

There is an interesting Irish angle to this proposal. Bishop Philbin was listed to speak in his own name. Since cardinals had precedence he was down the list and did not get his opportunity until three days later, 6 December. He would have prepared and submitted his text some days in advance. While his text lacked the clarity and conciseness of Cardinal Suenens's presentation, he made the same proposal. He would have suggested that there be two parts to the one document, rather than two separate documents. Given this contribution and others he made to the Council it is easy to conclude that the Irish bishops made a serious mistake in not asking him to oversee their preparation for the Council and their input into the discussion and drafting of the texts.

Obviously there were many other special moments during that first session that impacted on the development of the Council. I will just mention one, since it underlined how closely Pope John was following all that happened. He did not attend the daily sessions but followed many of them on close-circuit television. Lacking an effective closure procedure the debate on the Liturgy became very repetitious. A number of bishops had come to the Council intent on speaking. One such was Bishop Cule of Mostar in Yugoslavia. His talk did not address the particular section of the decree on the Liturgy that was being discussed but focused on his wish to have St Joseph's name included in the Canon of the Mass.

Cardinal Ruffini was chairing this session – by far the most effective chairman among the ten Presidents – and soon lost patience. He thanked him for his 'most pious sermon' and asked him to conclude. He ignored this request and Cardinal Ruffini asked him a second time. By this stage there was much amusement in the hall. He ignored him again and on the third occasion the Cardinal cut off his microphone. While the exchange may have amused the bishops in the hall it annoyed Pope John. He knew the bishop and knew that he had been imprisoned and tortured by the Nazis and having survived this received the same treatment from the communists when they took over. His torture and imprisonment caused deafness and he did not hear the requests asking him to finish. A few days later the Pope ordered the inclusion of St Joseph in the Canon of the Mass.

While many of these key moments occurred in the first session of Council there were also notable days in the remaining sessions. By the start of the second session in the autumn of 1963 there was a new Pope, Paul VI, the procedural rules and the chairing of the Council had been radically changed, the number documents for discussion at the Council greatly reduced and there was much greater clarity about where it was heading.

One poignant moment was the day Archbishop Slipyj addressed the Council. As Archbishop of the Greek-Catholic Church in the Ukraine he had spent twenty years in a Soviet gulag, the Church having been suppressed by the Communist regime in Russia. Pope John had secured his release. He spoke at length as, I suppose, he was entitled to do having been silent for so long. The content of his talk, however, caused great unease as he was pleading that a new Patriarchate be established for the Greek-Catholic Church in Ukraine. It was fascinating to watch the impassive faces of the observers from the Russian Orthodox Church during this talk. The tribune of the Observers from the other Churches was close to our own desk.

One of the finest of all the presentations made during the course of the Council was that made by Archbishop Parente on Chapter 3 of the Constitution on the Church, the chapter that dealt with collegiality. He was speaking on behalf of the Commission for Doctrine. His ease and fluency in Latin (a generation of Irish College students would have had him as their lecturer in dogmatic theology at the Lateran University) and the clarity of his presentation made a major impact on this debate. His successor as professor of dogmatic theology in the Lateran, Mgr Piolanti, himself a brilliant lecturer, called this the 'great betrayal'.

Another fascinating day centred on the debate on the decree on Religious Liberty, a contentious topic. When Archbishop Felici, the Secretary General, announced that discussion on this text was being postponed to the following year a real rumpus started in the Council Hall. Petitions to the Pope were handed around and over 1,000 signatures gathered in a couple of hours. Three cardinals then marched off around mid-day to meet with the Pope asking that this decision be reversed. The discussion on the draft text took place the following year as they discovered Pope Paul was not for changing. The final document was much the better for this delay, as many bishops, not least those from Eastern Europe who had suffered so much for the Church and had their freedom to practice their faith removed, were unhappy with the overly American content and context of the text.

A Few Observations

I will end with just a few observations. An event like an Ecumenical Council needs to find people of special charisms and talents if it is to succeed. This was certainly true of the *periti* (experts in theology, scripture, canon law etc.) appointed to be part of the Council process. Some of the more notable names, such as Fr Hans Kung and Fr Karl Rahner, made little or no contribution to the drafting and constant redrafting of the texts. It was backbreaking work and those most involved worked very long hours. The three most notable in this respect were Mgr Gerard Philips, Louvain, Fr Yves Congar OP, France and Fr Henri de Lubac SJ, Switzerland. It is interesting to note that an encyclical letter entitled *Humani Generis* (False Trends in Modern Teaching) published by Pius XII in 1950 was interpreted as censuring both Fr Congar and Fr De Lubac. Both were appointed cardinals later in life.

As I said earlier, if the Council Pius XII was planning had taken place it would have been a very different experience for the Church both then and since. It is good that Fr

Congar in his Journal of the Council speaks of Mgr Philips as the 'father of the Council', a tribute well merited since his input into the final documents was enormous. Sadly the workload he had to carry undermined his health and he died a couple of years after the end of the Council.

One regrettable aspect of the Council was the tendency to report its proceedings in simplistic terms – dividing the bishops into liberal (good) and conservative (bad). Many of the commentaries published in its immediate aftermath fell into this trap, as indeed did some prominent *periti* who preferred to spend their time speaking to media and others rather than becoming involved in its demanding and painstaking work. It was a distortion of what took place at the Council. One conclusion I came to from observing the scene over the four years was that those who professed themselves 'liberal and progressive' were much more rigid in their views and generally deaf to the arguments that the 'conservatives' made. I am not too sure that much has changed in this regard both within the Church and in society.

The final comment I would offer is that the great interpreter of the Council was the late Pope John Paul. In the immediate aftermath of the Council there were many contending voices on what the Council meant for the Church. When people did not find support in the documents they appealed to the spirit of the Council, that being whatever they wished to make it. Pope John Paul put the documents of the Council at the heart of his teaching as Pope, recognising that its influence on the life and mission of the Church will be felt for many decades and even centuries to come. It was in truth a gift to the Church.

It needed a holy man, Bl. John XXIII, of courage and determination to bring it into being. Over the five days he lay dying worldwide attention was focused on him. Before he died he offered his suffering and death for the Church and for the successful completion of the Council. This offering made it incumbent on his successor to continue the project. In Pope Paul VI the Church found a Pope totally committed to the Council, one endowed with acute theological expertise and a painstaking attention to detail that enabled him to successfully complete the task.

We can easily overlook that this was the first Council that drew its membership from every corner of the world. It articulated teaching on the Church's self-understanding, the Church at prayer, the fulfilment of the mandate of Christ to proclaim the Gospel to all nations, the outreach to other Churches and other Faiths, the proclamation of Gospel values on belief, on life, on peace etc. It was truly a gift to the Church that over time will be viewed as a major watershed in its life.

Gaudium et spes:
The Church in the Modern World

Most Rev. Diarmuid Martin

It is said that you will never get a committee to write a good document. *Gaudium et spes*, unlike most other Conciliar documents, was singularly favoured perhaps because it was not written by a Commission, but by two Commissions.

The Pastoral Constitution on the Church in the Modern World is a document which for many is emblematic of what Vatican II was about. The document envisaged a new style for the life of the Church. And yet in another sense it is untypical of Vatican II.

It was not envisaged in the preparatory period for the Council to have a document on the Church in the Modern World. *Gaudium et spes* did not grow out of a preparatory document, as was the case with the other major Conciliar documents. It took up some of the themes of early drafts on social action and Christian moral order, but is quite different to them. It was written, as I said, by two Commissions: those on Theology and on the Apostolate of the Laity.

The tone of the document was new and striking. It did not wish to talk about the Church *and* the Modern World or the Church *speaking to* the Modern Word; it was even less a document about the Church *against* the Modern World. It was about the Church *in* the Modern World. In the colourful phrase of Cardinal Joseph Ratzinger, *Gaudium et spes* was 'a kind of counter Syllabus'.

To achieve its task *Gaudium et spes* had to use a language that was different to that of traditional ecclesiastical documents – the language of dialogue. While I think that we can say it was quite successful in that use of a language of dialogue, it was not able to pass that style on to the mainstream of successive Vatican document-writers. I would dare say that one exception to that rule is the series of Messages for the World Day of Peace. I can say as an insider that this was not always easy. The Pontifical Council for Justice and Peace was responsible for presenting each year to the Pope the theme for the World Day of Peace and suggesting the outline for a text. We had to fight constantly to maintain the originality that Paul VI had wanted to give that celebration and which Pope John Paul II wished to maintain.

Paul VI chose 1 January for the World Day of Peace because it was not particularly a religious feast, but a day on which many people around the world naturally looked towards a future of new hope. He wished that the Message be addressed to people beyond the boundaries of the Church, though in a language which unmistakably sprung from the Christian religious heritage. In many ways this was the spirit of *Gaudium et spes*.

Within the Overall Understanding of the Church

Gaudium et spes was an untypical document of Vatican II and it used a language all its own. Yet it is not just an appendix to the Vatican Council. It belongs fully within the overall theological understanding of Church which inspired the documents of the Council. Suffice it to recall the opening paragraph of the Constitution on the Church *Lumen gentium*: 'Christ is the light of humanity and it is the heartfelt desire of the Council to bring to all humanity the light of Christ'. The Church is portrayed as being 'in Christ, in the nature of a sacrament – a sign and instrument – of communion with God and of unity among all'. Constantly, *Gaudium et spes* stresses the unity of this dual ministry of the Church: that of 'spreading the light of the Gospel throughout the world and uniting all people of whatever nation, race or culture in one spirit' (n. 92). And it recalls that 'the conditions of the modern world lend greater urgency to this duty of the Church of bringing all humankind to fuller union in Christ', 'for, while people of our present day are drawn more closely together by social, technological and cultural bonds, it still remains for them to achieve full unity in Christ'.

The Second Vatican Council understands the church as 'the universal sacrament of salvation'. The Church has through God's grace the dual task of working for the realisation of its own full unity and thus becoming a more effective sign of the unity of a fragmented humanity.

Gaudium et spes also makes more explicit and concrete the eschatological nature of the Church, stressed in *Lumen gentium*. The Church is God's pilgrim people on the way towards the final realisation of God's kingdom, when the human race as well as all of creation, will be perfectly re-established in Christ. God is preparing a new dwelling and a new earth, but as *Gaudium et spes* stresses, 'far from diminishing our concerns to develop this earth ... the expectancy of a new earth should spur us on' (n. 39).

It is appropriate that we should be remembering *Gaudium et spes* during Advent. Advent is a time that recalls for the Christian the mission to renew the creation. It is the season of Christian hope. Pope Benedict XVI in a recent Angelus Message recalls precisely how *Gaudium et spes* interprets every aspect and every element of human life and society: the family, culture, political and international community in the light of Christ.

The foundation of the church's role in the world is theological and Christological. In the Old Testament, God's intervention in history is perceived against the background of God being the creator and lord of all things. In the New Testament, especially in the writings of Saint Paul, sovereignty is attributed to Christ who is the head of the church and of all things.

The foundation of the restoration of all things has been laid in Christ. We must pray and wait for God to transform the world. Our Advent 'be awake', 'be alert' means that Christians are called to cooperate concretely, impatiently, restlessly in God's work of transforming the world. Christians have the duty and responsibility to establish a world order in conformity to God's gift of truth and grace received in Christ Jesus our Lord.

Just as Jesus is sent by the Father 'to bring the good news to the poor, to proclaim liberty to captives and to the blind new sight, to set the downtrodden free and to proclaim the Lord's year of favour', so Christians generation after generation are called to listen to the word of God in fresh ways in order to contribute through the instrumentality of the church towards the realisation of the kingdom in our time.

Gaudium et spes reminds us, however, that we must distinguish earthly progress clearly from the progress of the kingdom. This means that the dialogue between Church and world must be a dialogue of discernment.

Evaluating *Gaudium et spes* Forty Years On

How then do we evaluate *Gaudium et spes* forty years on? What have been the fruits of this dialogue for the Church and for society? What is the future direction of such a dialogue?

There are some who would say that the 'shelf life' of *Gaudium et spes* was by its nature short-lived and limited by the change in world situations. Others would say that through its own affirmation of 'the rightful autonomy of earthly things' the further evaluation of the Pastoral Constitution would be determined by developments in the social and economic sciences just as much as by theological or pastoral interpretations.

The Special Session of the Synod of Bishops in 1985, on the occasion of the twentieth anniversary of the Vatican Council looked at the ways in which *Gaudium et spes* had been interpreted over the years. In 1985, some felt that Pope John Paul II had called the Synod to launch a programme of going back on the Council. Quite to the contrary, the 1985 Synod clearly reaffirmed the Pastoral Constitution and its value, but qualified some questions regarding the context out of which *Gaudium et spes* arose.

The final document of that Special Session of the Synod noted with clarity: 'The Church as communion is a sacrament for the salvation of the world ... In this context we affirm the great importance and timeliness of the Pastoral Constitution *Gaudium et spes*'. The document then adds: 'At the same time, however, we perceive that the signs of our time are in part different from the time of the Council, with greater problems and anguish ... This requires a new and more profound theological reflection in order to interpret these signs in the light of the Gospel'.

Whether one agrees with its particular diagnosis or not, the 1985 Synod clearly recognised the particular genius of *Gaudium et spes*, namely fostering an ongoing process of dialogue between the Gospel message and the signs of the times, as an interaction in which the Church turns to the Gospel to help discern the signs of the times as each generation passes.

The verification, forty years after Vatican II, of the application of *Gaudium et spes* and of what form of *aggiornamento* it has brought to the Church is more difficult than with other Council documents. It can only be done within the context of developments in both Church and contemporary society and of their interaction. The process of evaluation must take into account the fact that the pace of social change in these forty years has been way beyond anything that the authors of the document could have foreseen.

Gaudium et spes (n. 5) speaks about the 'upheavals' which society at the time had to address. It noted that society was moving from a 'static to a dynamic and evolutionary conception of things'. But it still looked at the development of an industrial society and it was impossible at the time even to imagine what a post-industrial world would look like or the effects that an information revolution and a global knowledge-based economy would have on our society.

If the document underestimated the pace of change in society, it probably underestimated even more the changes that would take place in the Church, many of which *Gaudium et spes* itself provoked. The world and the Church of today have changed so much since the 1960s. *Gaudium et spes* predates 1968! And by 1968 I think both of the student revolt and of the publication of *Humanae Vitae*. It predates the fall of the Central and Eastern European communist regimes. It predates the era of globalisation. The question inevitably arises as to whether *Gaudium et spes* is as relevant to today's world as it was at the time of its publication.

The most important change in contemporary society since the publication of *Gaudium et spes,* and the one which requires most attention, concerns anthropology, the vision of the human person that is the driving force of contemporary reflection. At the time of the publication of *Gaudium et spes* there was a certain optimism in the air about the possibility of creating a better future. The Council itself and the miracle that Pope John XXIII seemed to have achieved in ecumenical dialogue contributed to this optimism and it was in tune with this broader cultural optimism. This optimism was marked by more sustained economic recovery after the trials of the Second World War. It was the time of a baby boom. It was the time of decolonisation and the emergence of new states in Africa and around the world. It was the Kennedy era!

There has been a good deal of discussion in more recent times about the overall thrust of *Gaudium et spes* regarding the fundamental goodness or frailty of human nature itself. Many would say today that *Gaudium et spes* was over-optimistic about the human project or the capacity of humankind to ensure that the good would prevail. Others would say that it was society that was over-optimistic and that *Gaudium et spes* does indeed contain many *caveats* about the ambiguities of society and about the clash between good and evil.

The anthropology of *Gaudium et spes* is a Christocentric anthropology. The dialogue with contemporary culture must be one in which the message of Jesus Christ appears as the unique corner stone. The Church continues in its desire to understand and even learn from modern culture. However, only the redeeming power of Jesus is capable of overcoming the presence of sin and evil in the world.

The 1985 Synod addressed this question in terms of the Mystery of the Cross:

> It seems to us that in the present-day difficulties God wishes to teach us more deeply the value, the importance and the centrality of the cross of Jesus Christ. Therefore the relationship between human history and salvation is to be explained in the light of the paschal mystery. Certainly the theology of the cross does not at all exclude the theology of the creation and incarnation, but, as is clear, it presupposes it. When we Christians speak of the cross, we do not deserve to be labeled pessimists, but rather found ourselves upon the realism of Christian hope.

Gaudium et spes was a careful document. For the Council the human condition always remains 'enigma' (n. 18). The document contains many of the *caveats* that some of its critics seem to have ignored. The optimism of *Gaudium et spes* is certainly captivating. Its cautionary tones were often, however, played down. I think of the many bishops who have taken *Gaudium et spes* as their motto but I have yet to meet one who has taken as his motto the second phrase of the opening sentence of the Pastoral Constitution: *Luctus et Angor* ('Grief and Anxiety').

Gaudium et spes itself is more realistic than some of its interpreters or interpretations. In many ways this is due to correctives introduced during the writing of the document, particularly by bishops from the German-speaking lands who had experienced how human nature and the minds of people could be deviated into the most extraordinary evil enterprises, such as was that of the holocaust. *Gaudium et spes*, indeed, from its first paragraph onwards draws attention to the ambivalence of human history, 'enslaved to sin' and marked by both the 'triumphs and disaster' of the enterprise of humankind. It takes up the famous words of the Letter to the Romans: 'Man weak and sinful often does what he would prefer not to do and fails to do what he would he like' (n. 10).

Where Do We Stand Today?

Forty years onwards, where do we stand? These forty years have seen enormous scientific progress. But war has continued: we still have large nuclear arsenals; we have had the Rwandan genocide; a brutal war in the heart of Europe in the Balkans; we have had continuous wars right across Africa; brutal forms of terrorism and hostage-taking have exploded on the world scene; economic, social and sexual exploitation have continued; hunger and malnutrition are still a problem; international law is under threat; and the dominant place of the person in the world economy is challenged in new ways.

Christians should be in the forefront in the working for a better world in these new circumstances. They should work with all those who share the same concern. But they must be careful to avoid the superficial and the clichéd. Their commitment must be coherent. It must not be limited to the occasional outburst of global solidarity such as that on the occasion of the Tsunami or the more militant enthusiasm engendered around meetings of the G8 meeting, the UN General Assembly or the WTO Ministerial Conferences. For the Christian, solidarity should be the stuff of every day. The anthropology of *Gaudium et spes* is one which demands solidarity as an imperative and not an option, a daily imperative and not an occasional awakening of conscience.

Christian comment on and commitment within society must be rooted in a truly Christian understanding of the human person that includes the reality of human sinfulness and therefore of the redeeming message of Jesus. Today so many people do not feel the need for redemption. The Christian believer must be fully present in the human enterprise, bringing to it that special discernment which springs from the irreplaceable light of Christ. Being present within the human enterprise is part of the calling to be a Christian.

In the aftermath of *Gaudium et spes* a new type of 'anonymous Christianity' appeared. It was not the theological anonymous Christianity of the non-Christian who espouses but not explicitly the values of the kingdom. It was an 'anonymous Christianity' among Christians, whose presence in social life was constructed deliberately without any specific reference to the Christian roots of his or her presence.

On the other hand, we have seen new forms of Christian fundamentalist presence in society and politics, which seem to say that our faith gives us a direct answer to every contemporary challenge. I believe that Catholics are under-represented in the religious right in the United States because of the effects of the teaching of *Gaudium et spes*, which recognises that the Word of God has to be mediated within the realities of the world through human reflection and the human sciences.

This does not mean that the individual Christian – or Church organisation for that matter – should be involved in the work of human advancement just alongside others, especially where there is no common anthropology or indeed where there is hostility to Christian anthropology.

The anthropology of *Gaudium et spes* is a theological anthropology. 'The human person is the only creature that God willed for its own sake' (n. 24), notes the Pastoral Constitution, using the single Council phrase most quoted by Pope John Paul II. It is that vision of human dignity rooted in a relationship with God, so beautifully stressed by Pope Benedict XVI in his inaugural address in Saint Peter's Square: 'Only when we meet the living God in Christ do we know what life is. We are not some casual and meaningless product of evolution. Each of us is the result of a thought of God. Each of us is willed, each of us is loved, each of us is necessary'.

In the intervening years since *Gaudium et spes,* dialogue between Church and the world has in many areas become more difficult, with an ever-increasing secularisation. The future presence of the Christian in society will be in a more and more pluralist society, at times less sympathetic to the role of religion. As opposed to the cultural climate at the time of the publication of *Gaudium et spes* there are many who no longer find it necessary to resort to religious principles to foster an ethic of solidarity. Many feel satisfied with a secularist understanding of what a more just world order offers them, without having recourse to the absolutes of religious belief. What is important is for all of us to keep dialogue and healthy debate within a mature, informed and non-ideological framework. The ability of Church and society to achieve such a framework and climate is an indication of the maturity of each.

The drop, finally, in religious practice in Western societies and the weakening among many young people of a real sense of religious culture means that many Christians no longer possess the theological and spiritual background necessary for a true discernment of the realities of the time. I will come back briefly to the question of formation for Christian social engagement.

A huge challenge in this dialogue around anthropology is the relationship between the individual human person and that of the human family, of humankind. The great temptation today is to read the concept of the human person in terms of current-day individualism, with all its ramifications, especially in terms of individual rights, individual attainment and individual fulfilment. *Gaudium et spes* attempts to show the interrelationship between the individual and their responsibilities in and for society. The danger is that the contemporary reader is unconsciously applying different interpretations of those terms than the Council itself would have done.

This challenge is most acute today, forty years after the publication of *Gaudium et spes*, in the area of marriage and the family. The dominant individualistic trends in philosophy and in popular culture go so far as to make it very difficult for many to fully comprehend the vision of marriage and the family that is to be found in the council document. The Church needs urgently to address the question of an *anthropology of human sexuality and marriage*, the 'first form of personal communion' (n. 12).

The economic realities of our time are very different to those at the time of the publication of *Gaudium et spes*. There has been a move away from a stress on the role of the State to one in which the positive aspects of the market and of human economic initiative are stressed, albeit with due reservations regarding the limits of the market. Once again anthropological issues are often at the heart of the debate. Pope John Paul II stressed the concept of a right to economic activity. This sprang from his view of the creativity and subjectivity present in the human person which gives rise also to a subjectivity of society. In a knowledge-based society the human person, human initiative and human creativity are the driving force of economic development.

Such a vision of economic development requires a new understanding of investing in human capacity. Poverty is the inability to realise God-given potential. Fighting poverty is above all about investing in people. It is about finding the ways – financial and technical – to ensure that people can realise their talents and improve their capacity. Perhaps the Church had not got it so wrong in the past when so much of its development work was in the field of education.

A challenge for the future is to develop a new vision of the preferential option for the poor. This means not just having general programmes for human advancement but ways in which those who are on the margins are brought as protagonists into the virtual circle of inclusion. The role of the Church in this situation is less that of wanting to be the voice of the poor and more that of ensuring that the poor have a voice. This means improving human capacity, but also broadening the appreciation of what it is to be human and moving away from a dominantly economic vision of society into one where a broader understanding of human purpose and hope can prosper.

The principle of *Gaudium et spes* concerning the universal destiny of the earth's resources is as important today as ever, especially in our analysis of the phenomenon of globalisation. Any form of globalisation which only increases exclusion has no title to call itself global. The goods of the earth today are not just land and capital, but knowledge and the fruits of human genius. We need to develop the fundamentals for a new era of solidarity within a knowledge-based society. We still have not been able to place the fruits of science fully at the service of the human community.

Gaudium et spes really never developed any reflections on the integrity of creation. This has been made up to some extent now by the rich teaching of Pope John Paul II. The *Compendium of the Social Doctrine of the Church* has brought together much of the biblical and magisterial teaching on this area. There is no necessary contradiction between a person-centered reflection on human realities and an ecological one. What is needed is to develop a vision that enhances, at the same time, the dignity of each human person, the unity of the human family and the integrity of creation. The ability to address and balance each of these three imperatives will be the key to economic and human development in the years to come.

War, Peace and the International Community

One of the most difficult discussions during the drafting of *Gaudium et spes* was on the theme of war. When I arrived as the Holy See's representative in Geneva, I presented my credentials to the then Head of the UN Office, a wise and wily former Soviet civil servant who had spent most of his time in disarmament work. He was regarded as belonging to the best of the old school: prudent and cautious yet aware of the realities of international insecurity.

I remember well that after a minimum of formalities we sat down and got straight into discussions on disarmament. He reminded me that he was personally involved in the negotiations of the principal International disarmament or arms control documents. And he said: 'Let us be clear these are all cold war documents, and they are becoming less and less adequate to the international situation today. But we have a potential disaster scenario before us. There is an inability or unwillingness to work towards new arms-control frameworks and at the same time the edifice of existing documents is beginning to collapse'. There was both truth and wisdom in the insight of the old disarmament practitioner.

The number of nuclear weapons in today's world is fewer but the number of countries possessing or interested in having nuclear weapons is high. Yet at the recent UN summit it was impossible to come to agreement on even mentioning proliferations issues.

That said, most people killed in wars after the Second World War have been killed with conventional weapons, either high-tech conventional weapons or indeed very low-tech but reliable and sturdy weapons. Very little progress has been made in introducing sharper control of the movement of conventional weapons and indeed sales of such arms are considered in many cases an important factor in national economic interest.

Church peace movements had perhaps become too focused on the nuclear issue. As the Soviet–American ideological conflict abated and as people felt that a nuclear conflagration war was no longer imminent, the interest in peace questions lessened. It is easy to be against nuclear catastrophe, but to engage with the complex mechanisms of arms production and sales is not so easy. We need a strong peace movement within the Church, not just the witness of the pacifist, but also the mediation of those who can elaborate and evaluate an ethical framework for arms control and reduction.

Pope John Paul took the teaching on the uselessness of war and therefore of the inappropriateness of war as an instrument of resolving international tensions far further than any of his predecessors. He was unafraid to say this to the world and to individual world leaders. It would be important that this anti-war legacy of Pope John Paul be developed in the ever more complex systems of today.

This brings me to the question of the international community, which was addressed in the final pages of *Gaudium et spes*. I suppose that I have spent a great deal of my life working in what is called the 'international community', but I have always affirmed that the international community does not exist, or that it exists only in a very embryonic state. States still make up the backbone of international relations. International organisations are made up of member states that act normally on the basis of the primacy of national interest. Even within the most evolved form of international co-operation ever known, namely the European Union, national interest can still be a major driving force for its members. International conventions are ratified by states. They relinquish their own sovereignty voluntarily – but in most cases not definitively and more and more often states are prepared to ignore obligations assumed or defy internationally recognised norms.

Global realities and interests exist today more than ever. But we do not have adequate governance structures to cope with the political and economic interests involved. International norms, like any other system of norms and laws, are there primarily to protect the weak and to curb the arrogance of the powerful.

There has been progress towards the elaboration of certain norms that constitute international law, but there are few sanctions available to apply to those that do not respect that law, particularly if the non-respect is by powerful nations (and, let me be clear, I am not speaking of the United States alone). In this context, the World Trade Organisation – despite all its imperfections – is perhaps one of the most advanced organisations in this area in that it has shown that it can tackle large as well as small offenders.

Honouring the Spirit of *Gaudium et spes*

How can the Church renew today the process that *Gaudium et spes* set in action, a renewal in the application of gospel principles to a reading of the signs of the times?

One way is to renew the social teaching of the Church, and the recent publication of a *Compendium of the Social*

Doctrine of the Church (2005) is an important sign. But it is important to remember that the social teaching of the Church is not a catalogue of readymade answers to the problems of our times. Paradoxically, the concept of the social teaching in the Church seemed to enter into crisis in the years immediately after Vatican II. Many were unhappy with the term doctrine, preferring social teaching or social reflection or social thought. There were clashes with different visions of social teaching. The cold war inevitably led to a polarisation of ideologies in social and economic reflection of all types. Certain trends of liberation theology had assumed a methodology that was flawed by elements of Marxist analysis. In other cases there was confusion between social teaching and outright political manifestos.

The *Compendium* sets out to offer a theological reading of the signs of the times. It examines the evolution of the revelation of God's love in the history of salvation, especially the revelation of God's Trinitarian love. It presents a unified corpus of principles and criteria that draw their origin from the Gospels and are applied to the realities of the times in order to help Christians to make their own responsible judgements on the best manner in which to stimulate the ideals proposed by the Gospel in contemporary culture. It aims to foster a dialogue with the social sciences and to bring the social thought of the scriptures into conversation with the dynamics of contemporary social life and culture.

At the same time the term 'doctrine' draws attention to the fact that the Christian cannot simply decide that 'anything goes' in terms of social conscience. It serves to remind all of us that certain underlying principles of the social doctrine, especially those closest to the kernel of the Church's teaching, have binding character in their own right. This principle should influence Christian legislators in the way they make laws. It should influence Christian citizens in the way they vote.

The Social Doctrine of the Church is above all an instrument to guide the formation of the consciences of Christian lay persons. Even though the *Compendium* is addressed first of all to bishops, I would venture to say that the success of the renewal of the social teaching of the Church in the years to come is not to be measured in the number of Episcopal statements on social issues – many of which of course may indeed be opportune – but in the maturity of the commitment and responsibility by which lay Christians involve themselves in the realisation of a more just and loving society, coherent with gospel principles.

For me, perhaps the principal challenge we have to face if we want to renew the spirit of *Gaudium et spes* in the Church of tomorrow is that of fostering the specific vocation of lay Christians in the secular sphere, of people who enter public life and service out of a spirit of dedication to the community and the common good. We need a new generation of articulate lay Christians who are prepared to take the dialogue initiated at Vatican II into a new and changing world and to engage every aspect of the culture of that world, economic, political and social. Mater Dei, I believe, is an institution that can play an important role in that process of formation.

People, Synod and Upper Room: Vatican II's Ecclesiology of Communion

Brendan Leahy

A Council about God

A straightforward question often gets to the heart of an issue. One such question was that put by Pope John XXIII to the bishops worldwide, the Roman authorities and Catholic universities as he convened the Second Vatican Council: 'Tell me what it should be about.' He received 8,972 proposals, wishes and requests![1] It is clear, therefore, that there were many ideas floating around as the Council began. Nevertheless, it is commonly accepted that the Church itself was the underlying concern.[2]

There were a number of reasons why this was the case. Firstly, the unfinished business of the First Vatican Council needed to be concluded. That council had been prematurely interrupted due to the 1870 Franco-Prussian war, with the result that its document on the Church, *Pastor Aeternus*, had ended up limited to only one isolated chapter on papal infallibility. The time had come for something more extensive.

Secondly, something new was rising on the ecclesial horizon – a new sense of Church. It could be seen in the writings of theologians belonging to various Church denominations. The Catholic theologian Romano Guardini talked about the Church awakening in people's souls; the Lutheran bishop, Otto Dibelius, wrote that the twentieth century would be the 'century of the Church' and the Reformed Church's theologian, Karl Barth, had achieved acclaim in his production of the theological series entitled *Church Dogmatics*. Barth epitomised a move within the Protestant tradition of the first half of the twentieth century away from a more individual-centred perspective of liberal theology to a new existential and theological recognition of the Church community as a living organism.

It is for these reasons that it is assumed that the Church was the main horizon in the bishops' mind as they approached the Council hall. Nevertheless, at a congress in 2000, the then Cardinal Joseph Ratzinger, prefect of the Congregation for the Doctrine of the Faith, offered a stimulating alternative perspective as he recounted his personal recollection of preparations for the Council he had attended as a young theologian.[3] His is an authoritative contribution, both in terms of his own first-hand experience of the Council and his role in its subsequent reception, not least in his becoming Pope in the year of celebrations marking the fortieth anniversary of the Council's conclusion.

In his paper he shared something told him by Cardinal Frings, whom he accompanied to the Council as theologian adviser. Like many others, in their preparatory deliberations the German bishops were beginning to focus on the topic of Church as *the* issue for the Council. Cardinal Ratzinger recalls Cardinal Frings telling him, however, that at a certain point during the German bishops' discussions, the then elderly but much-esteemed Bishop Buchberger of the diocese of Regensburg offered his advice. His simple suggestion cut ice. 'My brothers,' he said, 'at the

Council you must above all talk about God. This is what is most important.'

That Buchberger's words had an impact is no surprise. After all, it was he who had the idea of the much-applauded ten-volume German theological series *Lexikon für Theologie und Kirche*. As a result of this impact, an interior restlessness stirred at least within Cardinal Frings during the Council who constantly asked himself how he could satisfy this imperative. Indeed, in reaction to the first draft of the document on the Church, Frings was one of the bishops who asked that further attention be devoted to the mystery and the eschatological dimensions of the Church.

Summing up, Cardinal Ratzinger's own view is that:

> The Second Vatican Council certainly did intend to subordinate what it said about the Church to what it said about God and to set it in that context; it intended to propound an ecclesiology that was theological in the proper sense. The way in which the Council's teaching has been received, however, has hitherto overlooked this determinative prefix ... people ... have thus fallen short of the great overall perspectives of the Council Fathers.[4]

The contention that Vatican II's perspective was strongly God-centred can be backed up by other observations too. Already in Pope John XXIII's opening address at the Council (to which Paul VI referred again at its conclusion as he noted the Council's 'religious' intention[5]), we find a clear underlining of the primacy of God as the horizon of their deliberations, albeit while also underlining the anthropological focus. In referring to Jesus' words 'Seek first the kingdom of God and His justice', the 'Good Pope' commented that 'the word "first" expresses the direction in which our thoughts and energies must move'.[6]

From his study of the conciliar statements, it is also Walter Kasper's judgement that 'the question about the Church is subordinate to the question about God'.[7] In the above-mentioned paper, Cardinal Ratzinger noted the fact that the document on liturgy, the first conciliar document to be approved, reveals a conciliar architecture that places worship of God as its foundation stone. It is revealing too that the Council's document on the Church in the modern world, *Gaudium et spes*, contains a section that has been called a milestone in that, for the first time in a major Church document, the topic of the various forms of unbelief, indifference to and rejection of God in our times was addressed.[8] The first chapter of the document on inter-religious dialogue, *Nostra aetate,* emphasises the search for God and the ultimate questions found in every human heart.[9]

Communicating God
If we can take it that the Council strove to speak above all of God, it is legitimate for us to ask, 'What did it say about God?' It would, however, take us too far off the mark here to delve into that,[10] but at least a few brush strokes of a description are necessary inasmuch as it relates to the specific theme of this article.

It can be stated briefly that, as a central part of its 're-sourcing', the Council drew our eye to the biblical perspective on God. In underlining the role of Scripture as the soul of the Church, the document on divine revelation, *Dei verbum*, encouraged a deeper penetration of the biblical record of God's self-communication.

Both the document on divine revelation, *Dei verbum*, and the Council's dogmatic constitution on the Church, *Lumen gentium*, present a picture of God that is very definitely not the distant, remote, monadic God of deism, a God that is beyond the stars, but rather the God who has entered into our history, made our history his own and journeyed among us. It is the God who has initiated a dialogue and increasingly communicated his identity and life to us, promising us a future. It is the triune God, the communitarian God, the God of the story of love that we call the history of salvation. In his encyclical letter written forty years later, Pope Benedict XVI has again encouraged us to reflect more profoundly on this basic definition: God is Love (*Deus Caritas Est*).

In reviewing the causes of the contemporary rejection of God, the Council saw that the Church's own teaching and life had in ways contributed to the rejection of belief in God. Put simply, preaching and teaching about God as well as our living out of this belief in love has not always been up to the Gospel mark. This is hinted at here and there again by Pope Benedict XVI in his encyclical letter.[11]

Perhaps unwittingly, catechesis or preaching often presented a salvation merely beyond this world, or a God concerned only in one's individual relationship with him, or a God whose very existence seemed to threaten human freedom, autonomy and self-realisation, almost a one-personed monarchic God whom we might know of or know about, but not know as Love. And yet what matters most for Christians is the fact that we really share intimately in God's living, personal, merciful and freeing mutual (or, in more technical Trinitarian terms, *perichoretic*) life of love.

The Second Vatican Council wanted to re-present this true face of God shining in the life of the Church. So when it came to the issue of how to do so, it was no surprise that the Council's bishops emphasised the notion of the Church as *communion*. This is the Church's fundamental dimension that most reflects the triune, dialogical, community-mystery of God, the mutually giving, receiving, being-for-one-another God.

It has to be admitted that whatever about the centrality of the theme of communion at the Council, it was above all the theological notion of 'people of God' that initially gained most attention, with chapter two of *Lumen gentium* carrying this very title.[12] To capture something of the ecclesial mystery, the Council referred to many of the over one hundred images used in the New Testament to describe the Church, especially the notions of the Body-Bride of Christ and Temple of the Holy Spirit. By singling out the image of Church as 'People of God', the Council wanted to bring out more clearly the Church's eschatological, pilgrim character. It also wanted to bring about a shift from seeing the Church primarily as a static organisation or body that gets things done or an external agency of sacramental activities, teaching structures and pastoral actions, to something much deeper, universal and all-embracing – a people of holiness, love, life and truth. This employment of the 'People of God' image followed on from a line of theological reflection that emerged in the period 1940–1960 after Pius XII's 1943 encyclical letter on the Church as the Body of Christ, *Mystici Corporis*.[13]

To communicate his own life, God 'needs' the people of the Covenant, his people, the Church, as the German biblical scholar Gerhard Lohfink puts it. We are a people called together by God and in God and for God's self-communication in Jesus Christ in the power of the Spirit.[14] We are a people born in God's plan for God's plan.

After the Council, there was much debate about the meaning of the notion 'People of God'. Walter Kasper summarises the misunderstandings:

First of all, the people of God (*laos tou theou*) was misunderstood in the sense of being a political association of people (*demos*). This led correspondingly to a demand for a democratisation of the Church. Then the word 'people' was interpreted to mean the 'ordinary, simple people', as distinct from the establishment. But as the council uses the phrase, the people of God ... means the organic and structured whole of the church ...[15]

As we have already pointed out, despite the prominence of the 'People of God' focus, communion was a central motif running throughout the ecclesiology of the Council. Literature around the time of the Council clearly had contributed to this.[16] In 1985 the Final Report of the Synod marking the twentieth anniversary of the conclusion of the Council underlined this more explicitly. In synthetic and authoritative fashion it stated that the ecclesiology of Vatican II is an ecclesiology of communion.

The notion of communion itself, however, has various levels of meaning in the Council's texts.[17] The Council refers primarily to the Church's origins in the mystery of communion that is rooted in the Triune God's life that opens up for us in Jesus Christ. Walter Kasper summarises:

... according to the council, the mystery of the church means that in the Spirit we have access through Christ to the Father, so that in this way we may share in the divine nature. The communion of the church is prefigured, made possible and sustained by the communion of the Trinity. Ultimately ... it is participation in the Trinitarian communion itself. The Church is, as it were, the icon of the Trinitarian fellowship of Father, Son and Holy Spirit.[18]

It is this perspective, as at once Trinitarian, Christo-centric and anthropological, that the Council wanted to keep before us. It presented the Church as that realm of communion where, through the Crucified and Risen Christ working in the power of the Spirit, the culture of the Resurrection takes root in humanity. Gathered 'in' the Risen Christ and 'in' the Spirit, as St Paul emphasised so often, the Church is a people whose 'law' is mutual love whereby humankind can 'see' Christ. In the Church we discover humanity's living space in the heart of the Father with the Holy Spirit as the divine atmosphere.[19]

This underlining of communion clarified how the Church, the People of God, is to be 'a sign and instrument, that is, of communion with God, and of unity among humankind'.[20] And the source and summit of this communion is the paschal mystery that is celebrated in the Eucharist.[21]

Forty Years Later

Almost forty years after the Council, Pope John Paul II reminded the Church as it began its third millennium of the conciliar emphasis on communion. In his apostolic letter, *Novo millennio Ineunte*, he affirmed frankly that superficial touch-up jobs are not enough to promote this conciliar vision. Something more is needed. His invitation to the Church was to 'launch into the deep', renewing the ecclesial fabric so that humanity can really 'see' Jesus Christ in our 'living the Trinity' (n. 29) by living relationships of communion with one another:

> To make the Church the home and the school of communion: that is the great challenge facing us in the millennium which is now beginning … Communion must be cultivated and extended day by

day and at every level in the structures of each Church's life. There, relations between Bishops, priests and deacons, between Pastors and the entire People of God, between clergy and Religious, between associations and ecclesial movements must all be clearly characterized by communion.[22]

Already, some years previously, in his 1988 apostolic letter on Laity, Pope John Paul wrote of the need to 'remake the Christian fabric of the ecclesial community itself' in order to mend 'the Christian fabric of society'.[23] In other words, it is not simply a question of re-arranging the fabric of the ecclesial community, but rather fashioning it in a new way. John XXIII said as much in his opening address at the Council: 'The substance of the ancient doctrine of the deposit of faith is one thing, and the way in which it is presented is another ...'[24]

Since we are in 'a new stage of the Church's journey', one marked by increased focus on the reality of communion and attention to structures that facilitate participation in that communion, we do well to watch for those signposts from the Council's teaching directing us how to proceed. It is important to do so in line with what Pope Benedict XVI calls the Council's '"hermeneutic of reform", that is, of renewal in the continuity of the one subject-Church which the Lord has given to us'.[25]

The Final Report of the 1985 Extraordinary Synod names the implication of the Council's teachings: 'Because the Church is communion there must be participation and co-responsibility at all of her levels'.[26] Such participation and co-responsibility are not just good practice in terms of organisational quality management. It is a question of rendering more visible the presence of the Risen Christ in the midst of his people gathered in communion in his name.

I would like to propose two themes that I believe require further theological attention in our reception of the ecclesiology of communion proposed by Vatican II. They seem to be directions indicated to us by the Spirit 'speaking to the Church' (cf. Rev 2:7) in the reception of the Second Vatican Council's ecclesiology of communion.

Vatican II and a Culture of Synodality

One route inaugurated by the Council and travelled since then has been the spreading of what might be called 'a culture of synodality'. The Council itself, after all, was a synod![27] And it revamped many synodal processes that have marked the life of the Church since the Council and will do so increasingly in the twenty-first century.[28]

Throughout the history of the Church the words for 'synod' and 'council' have been used interchangeably when describing representative assemblies of representatives of churches. There have been different nuances in the use of the words but generally the root meaning is similar.

The Greek word 'synodos' has a dynamic and process meaning. In a general sense, it means journeying along the same road, going together, being a group of people on a journey. In patristic Greek the word designated a meeting of Christians or simply Church. In Latin the word 'concilium' refers to a convoked assembly (con-calere). Etymologically, this Latin word recalls the Hebrew word for Church, 'qahal', which was translated in the Septuagint by the word 'ekklèsia' (ek-kaleo), the coming together of the assembly called by God. All of this tells us that conciliarity and synodality belongs to the very essence of the Church. We are a journeying assembly; we go *together* to God.

In a strict sense, synods or councils are assemblies held at particular moments in the life of the Church to decide on particular issues that have arisen. Examples are easily cited:

the Council of Nicea (325) where the divinity of Jesus was clearly affirmed in the context of the Arian controversy; the Council of Ephesus (431) where Mary was called 'theotokos', mother of God in the context of the Nestorian controversy; and the Council of Chalcedon (451) where Jesus' divinity and humanity, two natures in one person, were defined in the continuing context of confusion and dispute.[29]

While these assemblies are particular expressions within a general synodal process of ecclesial life, it is important to recall the Second Vatican Council's perspective of the pilgrim People of God, constantly journeying 'synodally' in a common life, worship and community.

While Vatican II does not address the topic of synodality directly (the word 'concilium' is mentioned 80 times and 'Synod' 136 times but the references are primarily to the event of the Council itself), and while the major debate of the Second Vatican Council revolved specifically around the theme of collegiality of the bishops, nevertheless, the fact of the Council and this focus on collegiality itself opened up a rediscovery of the Church's synodality.[30] Furthermore, Vatican II was the beginning of a greater synodal understanding of Church by suggesting the establishment of a series of consultative councils and bodies that were to revitalise the synodal way throughout the ecclesial fabric.

The development of a culture of synodality, of course, must be understood as in no way taking from the essential element of the hierarchical principle and Petrine ministry within Catholic ecclesiology, clearly re-affirmed in Vatican II. It should not be confused with conciliarism, the teaching that supreme authority in the Church lies with a General Council, a teaching rejected in Vatican I's doctrine of papal primacy and Vatican II's doctrine on the collegiality of bishops with and under the Pope. A true understanding of synodality in the reception of Vatican II should be a strengthening and deepening of appreciation of the Church's hierarchical principle by underlining aspects of ecclesial life that promote greater participation in the life of the Church. There are many profiles of the Church working in harmony with the office of Peter.[31]

On the universal level of Church, the Second Vatican Council called for the Synod of Bishops[32] and Episcopal conferences.[33] The *Motu proprio* implementing four of the Council's decrees, *Ecclesiae sanctae*,[34] set up institutional partners for bishops. A Priests Council was called for[35] and the desirability of Pastoral Commissions was expressed.[36] Mention was also made of a council of consultors.[37]

Councils involving lay people were advocated in the Decree on the apostolate of the Laity[38] with the recommendation that 'such councils should be found too, if possible, at parochial, inter-parochial, inter-diocesan level, and also on the national and international plane'.[39] Provision was made for better integration of religious into dioceses.[40] Likewise, *Ecclesiae Sanctae* provided for better integration of coadjutor and auxiliary bishops.[41]

Since the Council, within the Catholic Church, there have been definitive developments within this 'synodal' understanding of the Church.[42] There is renewed focus on *Lumen gentium*'s statement that it is 'in' the local churches and 'formed out of them' that the one and unique Catholic Church exists (*LG* 23).

On the universal level synods have taken place regularly in Rome. Pope John Paul II (an initiative Pope Benedict has continued) called Regional/continental synods. Many diocesan synods have been held throughout the Church and in 1997 an Instruction on Diocesan Synods was published by the Congregation for the Bishops and the Congregation for the Evangelisation of Peoples.

In 1998 the apostolic letter *Apostolos Suos* dealing with the theological nature and status of episcopal conferences was released. It followed considerable theological reflection on the nature of episcopal conferences in the previous fifteen years.

More immediately for most people, however, the websites of episcopal conferences and of dioceses indicate an array of commissions, committees and agencies whose membership expresses an increased participation of bishops, priests and religious, lay faithful, men and women in institutionalised synodal aspects of Church life at both regional and diocesan levels.

Impulses from Ecumenical Dialogue

The culture of synodality that is gaining ground within the Catholic Church in recent years is also, in part, thanks to ecumenical engagement initiated at Vatican II. In the 1995 document on ecumenicsm, *Ut Unum Sint* (May they all be One), John Paul II underlined the fruits that have emerged in the last forty years of ecumenical dialogue. It could be argued that one of these is the fact that through ecumenical day-to-day contacts with other churches and ecclesial communities, the concepts of 'council', 'conciliarity', 'conciliar communion' and 'synodality' have become more familiar words in the vocabulary of Catholic theology and reflection.[43] Indeed, the experience of synodality is one of those instances where the Catholic Church can learn from the practices of other churches.

Initially, in the doctrinal dialogues of the World Council of Churches, conciliarity was viewed as an ecumenical issue of strategy about how churches might relate. But in recent decades there is a growing recognition that it has to do with the fundamental structure of Church life itself. Conciliarity is increasingly viewed as an expression of the essentially communion character of the one Church of Jesus Christ. Here it is sufficient to rehearse just a few key developments.

Within the Orthodox Tradition, Russian theologians of the nineteenth century such as Khomyakov spoke of a qualitative notion of catholicity, a love-inspired 'unity in multiplicity'. Eventually the word 'sobornost' emerged to describe this conciliar-like nature of the Church's unity.[44] Sergius Bulgakov popularised the notion of the Church as 'sobor', meaning assembly, equivalent to conciliarity and synodality with the nuances of togetherness and mutuality. The American Orthodox theologian Alexander Schmemann has written of the Church that, 'all her life is conciliar because conciliarity is her essential quality'.[45]

In the Faith and Order Lausanne Conference of 1927 (n. 27) it was said that in the order of life of a reunited Church the episcopal, presbyteral and congregational systems would find a place. The foundation of the World Council of Churches in Amsterdam in 1948 was itself a highlighting of the notion of conciliarity. And various Assemblies of the World Council of Churches since then have focussed on the topic of conciliarity.

It suffices here to note the New Delhi Assembly in 1961 and the Uppsala Assembly of 1968 (the latter called for a universal council). The Nairobi Assembly in 1975 spoke of 'conciliar communion' as a reflection of the uni-triune nature of God in the life of the Church, while the Canberra Assembly of 1991 proclaimed the ecclesiology of communion (*koinonia*) as the fundamental concept of Christian unity and conciliarity.[46]

Of particular significance is the 1971 Faith and Order Louvain Report, the first report issued from this body after the Catholic members joined it in 1967. The Report contains a paper prepared by a committee on the theme 'Conciliarity and the Future of the Ecumenical Movement'.

One of the Catholic members at that Louvain gathering was the theologian, Joseph Ratzinger.

In the Report, conciliarity is defined as 'the coming together of Christians – locally, regionally or globally – for common prayer, counsel and decision, in the belief that the Holy Spirit can use such meetings for his own purpose of reconciling, renewing and reforming the Church, by guiding it towards the fullness of truth and love'.[47] It goes on to note that conciliarity:

> ... can find different expressions at different times and places. The ecumenical movement has both challenged and helped us to seek appropriate conciliar forms for our own time. Facing the questions of the contemporary world, and drawn together by a common desire to serve the Lord together in the whole life and mission of the Church, the Churches have been led in our own time to develop new forms of conciliarity – both within each Church, and in the councils of Churches at the local, national, regional and world levels. It is important that we should reflect upon this fact, should endeavour to relate it to the conciliar experience of the Church in the past, and should seek more adequate forms of conciliarity in our day.[48]

In the final part of the Report, it comments on the significance of the Second Vatican Council and states that it was:

> not only a conciliar event of epoch-making importance, but has also led to a ferment of discussion throughout the Roman Catholic Church on conciliarity, and to new experiments in conciliar practice at various levels of the Church's life.[49]

The World Council of Churches' Faith and Order Lima document, *Baptism, Eucharist and Ministry* (1982), nn. 26–7, points towards a synodal horizon as it underlines three dimensions of ordained ministry – personal, collegial and communitarian.

More recently, there have been three documents that also refer to a synodal approach in living the Church's communion. The 1998 World Council of Church, Faith and Order Paper entitled *Nature and Purpose of the Church* laid out a number of theological bases for the synodal understanding of the Church.

The 1998 ARCIC document entitled *The Gift of Authority: Authority in the Church III* looks specifically at 'Sinodality: exercise of authority in communion'. While suggesting a new Anglican appreciation of the universal Petrine ministry, it also recognises there has been a development of synodal structures in the Roman Catholic Church and an increased exercise of synodality at a local level, though it raises the question as to whether Roman Catholic Church clergy and lay faithful are sufficiently involved in the formation of synodal organisms at all levels.

In the Dombes Group's document, issued in 2005, *Un seul Maître: L'autorité Doctrinale dans l'Église*,[50] Catholic, Lutheran and Reformed theologians offer their reflection on a number of issues relating to authority in the Church. They point out that, while the Catholic Church has in its Tradition recognised synodality, it has emphasised, above all, the personal role of authority of the bishops in the local church and the Pope in the universal Church. It goes on to advocate an improvement in synodal structures, regularisation of synods, greater participation of the faithful in ecclesial responsibility and development of 'synodal culture' in local churches.[51] Interestingly, it also pointed out that the Reform and Lutheran Churches with their presbyteral-synodal and episcopal-synodal structures need to develop synodal structures at regional and national levels to ensure doctrinal communion and common decisions at this level and so give greater attention to the Church's tradition of faith and catholicity.

A Synodal Culture and the Church's 'Upper Room'

The need to promote a culture of synodality is one of the signposts along the journey of reception of the Second Vatican Council's ecclesiological focus on communion. But it is also the case that dissatisfaction has been expressed at how this synodal praxis has been realised.[52]

Several reasons have been put forward for this. On the one hand, it has been said that there's a lack of conviction on the part of pastors and persistent clericalism. The canonical framework is said to be weak. The promotion of a synodal culture requires greater catechetical formation. There is a need for further historical, liturgical and canonical research to re-discover, renew and expand in contemporary pastoral practice forms of synodality that already exist in the Church.

Nevertheless, before making practical plans, we would do well to recall the words of Pope John Paul: 'Ours is a time of continual movement which often leads to restlessness, with the risk of "doing for the sake of doing". We must resist this temptation by trying "to be" before trying "to do".'[53] Something more is needed than merely structural renewal. Promotion of a synodal culture is not just tweaking the system.

The *Group des Dombes* wrote on the need for spiritual conversion and renewal.[54] Walter Kasper too, to take but one theological representative, has written of the spiritual renewal and recovery of the dimension of mystery required in fostering greater participation in the life of the Church.[55]

But, most significantly, the Second Vatican Council itself provided a signpost that points this way of spiritual renewal in our reception of the Council's ecclesiology of communion. It amounts to what could be called a rediscovery of the 'Upper Room' aspect of the Church.

On the one hand, reference to the 'Upper Room', reminds us of the Eucharist which is at the heart of ecclesial communion. Cardinal Joseph Ratzinger writes that:

> 'Communion' ecclesiology is in its inmost nature a eucharistic ecclesiology ... In the Eucharist, Christ, who is present in bread and wine and is ever anew giving himself in them, builds up the Church as his body, and through his body that rises again he unites us with God the Trinity and with each other. The Eucharist takes place at whatever place is in question and yet it is at the same time universal, because there is only one Christ and only one body of Christ. The Eucharist includes the priestly ministry of *repraesentatio Christi* and, thereby, also the network of service and ministry, the coexistence of unity and multiplicity, which is already suggested in the term 'communion'. There is thus no doubt we can say that this concept carries in it an ecclesiological synthesis that links talk about the Church with talk about God and with living with God's help and living with God; a synthesis that comprehends all the essential points that the ecclesiology of Vatican II intended to express and correctly relates them to each other.[56]

As well as being associated with the Eucharist, however, the Upper Room is also noted in the Acts of the Apostles as the place of Pentecost (Acts 1:12; 2; cf. Jn 20:19-22). And it is well known that John XXIII and subsequent Popes associate

Vatican II with a new Pentecost in the Church. Pentecost is the great event of conversion where the apostles, who had been crushed by the crucifixion and death of Jesus Christ, were empowered to begin again to be and speak in Christ. It is the event that forms them immediately into a community of 'one heart and soul', living a communion of goods both material and spiritual (Acts 2:42; 4:32).

In his opening speech at the Council, Pope John XXIII made a direct comparison between the assembly of bishops in the Vatican Basilica and the Upper Room of Jerusalem. He expressed his hope that the Church was entering a new moment of her history, enabling her to go out again 'as if from a second apostolic upper room'. In his encyclical on the Holy Spirit, *Dominum et Vivificantem*, Pope John Paul II wrote that 'while it is an historical fact that the Church came forth from the Upper Room on the day of Pentecost, in a certain sense one can say that she has never left it. Spiritually the event of Pentecost does not belong only to the past: the Church is always in the Upper room that she bears in her heart' (n. 66).

The Holy Spirit brings the Son's mission to completion by transmitting to us the filial relationship with God that makes us brothers and sisters to one another: 'And because you are children, God has sent the Spirit of his Son into our hearts, crying, "Abba, Father!"' (Gal 4:6). A true promotion of a culture of synodality needs to listen to what the Spirit is saying to the Church today in terms of the spiritual renewal needed to give life to the ecclesiology of communion. A number of signs of this renewal can be pointed to:

a) There has been an increased magisterial and theological focus on a spirituality of communion as necessary for any true structural development within the Catholic Church. In 2001, Pope John Paul II wrote:

> ... we need *to promote a spirituality of communion*
> ... Let us have no illusions: unless we follow this
> spiritual path, external structures of communion will
> serve very little purpose. They would become
> mechanisms without a soul, 'masks' of communion
> rather than its means of expression and growth.[57]

The Pope goes on to outline the elements of a spirituality
of communion. It is our 'heart's contemplation of the
mystery of the Trinity dwelling in us, and whose light we
must also be able to see shining on the face of the brothers
and sisters around us'. It involves 'an ability to think of our
brothers and sisters in faith within the profound unity of
the Mystical Body, and therefore as "those who are a part
of me"'. It makes us 'able to share their joys and sufferings,
to sense their desires and attend to their needs, to offer
them deep and genuine friendship'. A spirituality of
communion implies also the ability 'to see what is positive
in others, to welcome it and prize it as a gift from God: not
only as a gift for the brother or sister who has received it
directly, but also as a "gift for me"'. Not least, a
spirituality of communion means 'to know how to "make
room" for our brothers and sisters, bearing "each other's
burdens"'.

Writing in the 1980s towards the end of his life, and in
commenting on the spirituality of the Church of the future,
Karl Rahner observed: 'I suspect that the element of a
fraternal, spiritual fellowship, of a communally lived
spirituality, can play a greater part and be slowly but
courageously acquired and developed.'[58]

He explained that it will not suffice to continue in an
individual-I-God-shaped spirituality dressed up in
community guise. Recalling the first Pentecost he noted
how it was 'a communal experience of the Spirit, clearly

conceived, desired and experienced in a general way' and that it was not 'an accidental local gathering of a number of individual mystics, but an experience of the Spirit on the part of a community as such'. It is such communal experience that needs to be witnessed to today. Paul VI's famous dictum: 'people today listen to witnesses more than to teachers and to teachers if they are witnesses' applies particularly to the Church's communitarian life.[59]

b) A second pointer from the Spirit has been the crescendo in reflection on the Church's charismatic profile or dimension. In *Lumen gentium* (n. 4) we read:

> Guiding the Church in the way of all truth (cf. Jn 16:13) and unifying her in communion and in the works of ministry, [the Spirit] bestows on her varied hierarchic and charismatic gifts, and in this way directs her; and he adorns her with his fruits (cf. Eph 4:11-12; 1 Cor 12:4; Gal 5:22). By the power of the Gospel he permits the Church to keep the freshness of youth. Constantly he renews her and leads her to perfect union with her Spouse. For the Spirit and the Bride both say to Jesus, the Lord: 'Come!' (cf. Apoc 22:17). Hence the universal Church is seen to be 'a people brought into unity from the unity of the Father, the Son and the Holy Spirit'.

This text reminds us that the Church is constantly being renewed and rejuvenated as it grows and matures in its desire for perfect union with Jesus Christ. The Spirit is the source of renewing charisms. And it is the Spirit who, in bringing about the unity of the Church, brings about the unity of these charisms in the Church (see 1 Cor 14:31 and 1 Cor 12:14-31). To each is given a manifestation of the

Spirit for the common good (1 Cor 12:37). Again in *Lumen gentium* (n. 12) we read:

> It is not only through the sacraments and the ministrations of the Church that the Holy Spirit makes holy the People, leads them and enriches them with his virtues. Allotting his gifts according as he wills (cf. Cor 12:11), he also distributes special graces among the faithful of every rank. By these gifts he makes them fit and ready to undertake various tasks and offices for the renewal and building up of the Church, as it is written, 'the manifestation of the Spirit is given to everyone for profit' (1 Cor 12:7). Whether these charisms be very remarkable or more simple and widely diffused, they are to be received with thanksgiving and consolation since they are fitting and useful for the needs of the Church.

Theological reflection on the significance of the prophetic/charismatic dimension of the Church has continued since the Council in authors such as Karl Rahner, Rind Fisichella and Yves Congar.

c) The Spirit, it seems, is today not only encouraging renewed doctrinal insight and reminding us of the charismatic and prophetic nature of the Church, but is also bringing to life new forms and 'laboratory-like' expressions of communion that are like indicators for the whole Church.

The German theologian, Medhard Kehl, indicates three main forms: 1) basic communities begun in and associated primarily with Latin America;[60] 2) small Christian communities that originated in and are to be found mostly in Africa;[61] and 3) new ecclesial movements that have universal extension.[62]

The rise and spread of new ecclesial movements and communities in the Church is a phenomenon that is gaining increased attention in magisterial teaching, pastoral consideration and theological reflection. For instance, at an unprecedented gathering of movements and new ecclesial communities together with the Pope at Pentecost in May 1998, Pope John Paul II spoke of the 'upper room in St Peter's Square'. He noted the Council's discovery of the charismatic dimension of the Church and went so far as to state the institutional and charismatic aspects are 'co-essential' to the Church's constitution.

In other words, he views the charisms that give rise to new forms of community life as contributing constitutionally to the renewal and sanctification of God's People:

> It is from this providential rediscovery of the Church's charismatic dimension that, before and after the Council, a remarkable pattern of growth has been established for ecclesial movements and new communities ... In our world, often dominated by a secularized culture which encourages and promotes models of life without God ... There is so much need today for mature Christian personalities, conscious of their baptismal identity, of their vocation and mission in the world! There is great need for living Christian communities! And here are the movements and the new ecclesial communities: they are the response, given by the Holy Spirit, to this critical challenge at the end of the millennium. You are this providential response.[63]

The fact that Pope Benedict XVI called together another gathering of ecclesial movements and communities in June 2006 is yet another underscoring of this new blossoming on the Church.

The Doorway

This paper would be incomplete without reference to the 'doorway' into the 'Upper Room' of the Church and its culture of synodality. That 'doorway' is Jesus crucified and forsaken on the cross. It is not insignificant that when the risen Jesus appeared to the disciples in the Upper Room, and before breathing the Holy Spirit upon them, he showed them his wounds (cf. Jn 20:20; 27). The resurrection and the emergence of the Church on Pentecost Day follow Jesus' death on a cross.

Here we come to the inner chamber of the Church as the People of God in synodal communion. Jesus crucified, who cried out 'why' on the cross, is the key not only to the redemptive value of suffering but also to building communion in correspondence to the divine gift of new life that has been bestowed on us. He had experienced the most extreme form of lack of communion with God and with the humanity with whom he had journeyed as fellow pilgrim.

In this 'mystery within the mystery'[64] of Jesus crucified and forsaken, we learn not just how to confront sufferings, but also how to live a communion of mutual love with one another as we journey 'synodally'. In pointing to him as the model, the New Testament directs us to learn from him how to inter-relate in synodal communion.

In John's Gospel we read, 'No one has greater love than this, to lay down one's life for one's friends' (Jn 15:13) and then the following chapters bring us into a meditation of Trinitarian-communion. The law of mutual love is not simply a moral imperative. It is, as *Lumen gentium* (n. 9) tells us, the 'law' of ecclesial communion and its key is 'laying down one's life'. Matthew and Mark spell that out in terms of Jesus' abandonment on the cross (Mt 27:46; Mk 15:34).

If I am to live communion and promote a synodal culture, I need to learn this 'living the Trinity'[65] as revealed in Jesus Christ at the supreme moment of his self-giving to God and to us. From him I learn that I cannot enter the heart of another person if my own spirit is filled with my richness in whatever form it takes – ideas, spiritual insight, plans or indeed burdens, disappointments, difficulties. In order to love my neighbour, I must constantly make myself so poor in spirit that I possess nothing but love. And love is emptiness of self. This is what we learn from Jesus crucified and forsaken.

And what we discover from him concerning relationships between individuals can also be said to apply to the relationships between parishes, dioceses, movements, associations and Church agencies.

That is why Paul writes in Phil 2:3-8: 'let the same mind be in you that was in Christ Jesus, who, though he was in the form of God, did not regard equality with God as something to be exploited, but emptied himself [*heautón ekénosen*], taking the form of a slave, being born in human likeness. And being found in human form, he humbled himself and became obedient to the point of death – even death on a cross'. Daniel Harrington writes: 'This text indicates the extent to which Paul ... valued the union of hearts and minds within the Christian community ... What is at stake is the Philippians' identity as Christians and their manner of dealing with one another within the community of faith.'[66]

In practical terms, the law of mutual love with the measure of Jesus' love right to the point of self-emptying and abandonment means opening ourselves in love to diversity of expressions and roles. It means not focusing only on our own Church body or group or personal inspiration. It also means taking onto ourselves the limits of others, and loving them even when their way disturbs my peace and light. Of course, it is also about giving all that we are, including the truth we possess. But offering it out of love. And this holds true in how we relate with the office holders within the institutional dimension of the Church.

A love like this 'wounds' but it conforms us to Jesus crucified and forsaken from whom the Spirit of communion poured out upon humanity.[67] This kind of love enables the gift of the Holy Spirit (which is the gift that Jesus crucified wants to give us) to circulate freely among us as in the first Upper Room.

It is this love that Pope Benedict has put before us again in his first encyclical. This love enables us to 'live the Trinity' as a people engrafted onto one another as Christ's mystical body, members travelling in synod towards the eternal life of heaven.

Conclusion

In this article, I have proposed that a major aim of Vatican II was to proclaim God anew for our time. In defining the Church as 'the People of God', the Council proposed an ecclesiology of communion as necessary for the renewal of the ecclesial fabric in order to present the true face of the triune God of Love. This ecclesiology is advancing in theological reflection, magisterial teaching and, not least, in new forms of ecclesial praxis. Its reception requires the promotion of a 'culture of synodality', but that in itself is not sufficient. It is important to be attentive to those signposts seen in the 'Upper Room' of the Church where we discern the Spirit underlining a spirituality of communion and deeper awareness of the Church's charismatic/prophetic profile.

Notes
1. See G. Philips, *La Chiesa e il suo mistero nel concilio vaticano II*, Milan: Jaca Books, 1967, p. 106.

2. See the informative commentaries such as *Unam Sanctam* series published by Cerf, Paris: *L'Église de Vatican II. Vols II and III* (1966); the five volume *Commentary on the Documents of Vatican II* edited by Herbert Vorgrimler, New York: Herder and Herder, 1967–1969; and a commentary edited by Kevin McNamara, *Vatican II: The Constitution on the Church. A Theological and Pastoral Commentary*, Chicago: Franciscan Herald, 1968.

3. The text of his address was first published as 'L'Ecclesiologia della Constituzione *Lumen gentium*' *Nuova Umanità* XXII (2000/3-4), pp. 383–407 and its English translation is to be found in 'The Ecclesiology of the Constitution, *Lumen gentium*' in Joseph Cardinal Ratzinger, *Pilgrim Fellowship of Faith: The Church as Communion*, San Francisco, 2005, pp. 123–152.

4. 'The Ecclesiology', pp. 125–126.

5. www.vatican.va/holy_father/paul_vi/speeches/1965/docu ments/hf_p-vi_spe_19651207_epilogo-concilio_en.html

6. John XXIII, Opening Address, in Walter M. Abbot, *Documents of Vatican II*, London: Geoffrey Chapman, 1967, p. 714.

7. See Walter Kasper, *Theology and Church*, London: SCM, 1989, p. 153.

8. See nn. 19–21.

9. Thomas Stransky, 'The Genesis of Nostra aetate', *America* 193, October 2005/12.

10. See Félix-Alejandro Pastor, 'Human Beings and their Search for God: The Doctrine of the Magisterium of the Church between Vatican I and Vatican II' in René Latourelle (ed.), *Vatican II: Assessments and Perspectives: Twenty-Five Years After (1962–1987)*: Volume II, New York: Paulist, 1988, pp. 367–385. See also Ghislain Lafont, 'La Constitution *Dei verbum* et ses précedents conciliaires' *Nouvelle Revue Théologique* 110 (1988), 58–73.

11. See nn. 3, 5, 18, 24, 27,

12. See Yves Congar, 'The Church: The People of God', *Concilium* (1965/1), pp. 7–19.

13. See Angel Antón *El Misterio del la Iglesia: Evolucion Historica de las Ideas Eclesiologicas. Vol II: De la apologética de la Iglesia-misterio en el Vatican II y en el posconcilio,* Madrid-Toledo: Catolica, 1987, and see also David J. Bosch, *Transforming Mission: Paradigm Shifts in Theology of Mission,* Maryknoll, N.Y.: Orbis Books, 1991, p. 390.

14. *Does God need the Church?* Collegeville, Minnesota: The Liturgical Press, 1999.

15. See Walter Kasper, *Theology and Church,* London: SCM, 1989, p. 162. See also the International Theological Commission, 'Selected Themes of Ecclesiology' in Michael Sharkey (ed.), *International Theological Commission, Texts and Documents, 1969–1985,* San Francisco: Ignatius Press, 1989, pp. 267–304. On postconciliar ecclesiology see Angel Antón, 'Postconciliar Ecclesiology: Expectations, Results, and Prospects for the Future' in René Latourelle (ed.), *Vatican II: Assessments and Perspectives: Twenty-Five Years After* (1962–1987): Volume I, New York: Paulist, 1988, pp. 407–438.

16. See Yves Congar, 'Notes sur les mots "confession", "eglise" et "communion"', in *Irenikon,* 23 (1950), pp. 3–36; 'De la communion des Eglises a une ecclesiologie de l'Eglise universelle', in Y. Congar and Bernard-D. Dupuy (eds), *L'episcopat et l'Eglise universelle,* Paris: Cerf, 1962, pp. 227–260; L. Hertling's work published on the eve of the Council in *Una Sancta* 17 (1962), pp. 91–125 and printed as *Communio: Church and Papacy in Early Christianity,* Chicago: Loyola University, 1972; Jerome Hamer, *The Church is a Communion,* New York: Sheed & Ward, 1964. These works contributed to Vatican II's communion ecclesiology. See Ratzinger, 'The Ecclesiology', p. 131, fn. 5.

17. See Congregation for the Doctrine of the Faith, 'Some Aspects of the Church understood as Communion' (*Communionis notio*), *Origins* 20 (June 25, 1992), pp. 108–112. See also an unsigned article on the first anniversary of *Communionis notio* in *L'Osservatore Romano* (English

edition), 4 July 1993, pp. 4 and 10. See also Avery Dulles, 'Communion' in Nicholas Lossky et al. (eds), *Dictionary of the Ecumenical Movement*, Geneva: WCC, 2002, pp. 229–232.

18. Kasper, *Theology & Church*, p. 152.
19. Cf., *Lumen gentium*, n. 9.
20. *Lumen gentium*, n.1
21. See the Constitution on the Sacred Liturgy, *Sacrosanctum concilium*, espec. 10.
22. Pope John Paul II's Apostolic Letter, *Novo millennio Ineunte* (6 January 2001), n. 43.
23. John Paul II, Post-Synodal Apostolic Exhortation, *Christifideles Laici* (30 December 1988) 34: *AAS* 81 (1989), pp. 393–521, espec. pp. 454–457.
24. Walter M. Abbott, *The Documents of Vatican II*, p. 715.
25. See Christmas address to the Roman Curia, 22 December 2005.
26. See The Final Report, II, c, 6.
27. Yves Congar, 'Konzil als Versammlung und grundsatzliche Konziliaritat der Kirche', in Herbert Vorgrimler (ed.), *Gott in Welt*, Vol. 2, Freiburg: Herder, 1964, pp. 135–165; and Y. Congar, 'The Conciliar Structure or Regime of the Church', *Concilium* 167 (1983), pp. 3–12.
28. See D. Staniloae, 'Dogmatische Grundlagen der Synodalität', *Ostkirchliche Studien* (Würzburg) 20 (1972), pp. 3–16; G. Alberigo, 'Synodalität in der Kirche nach dem Zweiten Vatikanum' in W. Geerlings and M. Seckler, *Kirche sein*, Freibourg, 1994, pp. 333–347; Christopher O'Donnell, 'Synod of Bishops' and 'Synod and Councils, Local' in *Ecclesia*, Collegeville: Liturgical Press, 1996, pp. 431–435; Terence L. Nichols, *That All May Be One: Hierarchy and Participation in the Church*, Collegeville, Minn.: Liturgical Press, 1997; Ghislain Lafont, *Imagining the Catholic Church: Structured Communion in the Spirit*, Collegeville, Liturgical Press, 2000, pp. 187–189; George Tavard, 'The Catholic Church as Conciliar Church' in *Priests and People* 14 (2000/1), pp. 3–7; S. Dianich, 'Sinodalità' in G. Barbaglio et al., *Teologia*, Milan:

San Paolo, 2002; Emmanuel Lanne, 'Conciliarity', in Nicholas Lossky et al. (eds), *Dictionary of the Ecumenical Movement*, Geneva: WCC, 2002, pp. 237–238; Libero Gerosa, 'Rechtstheologische Grundlagen der Synodalität in der Kirche. Einleitende Erwägungen', in W. Aymans-K-Th Geringer, *Iuri Canonico Promovendo Feschrift für Heribert Schmitz sum 65 Geburtstag* (Regensburg, 1994), pp. 35–55; '"Coltivare e dilatare gli spazi di comunione": Ambiti e Strumenti dell'ecclesiologia di comunione' *Path* 4 (2005), pp. 105–120; E. Corecco, 'Sinodalità' in *Nuovo Dictionario Teologico*, pp. 1431–1456; Giovanni Cereti, 'Chiesa e sinodalità' in *Il Regno-attualità* 18 (2005), pp. 591–593.

29. See the recognised collection of council proceedings and decisions of Johannes Dominicus Mansi, *Sacrorum conciliorum nova et amplissima collectio*, 53 vols, Arnhem and Leipzig: Verlag H. Welter, 1901–1927.

30. Collegiality emerged not least because Pope John XXIII had called for a renewed vision of the identity of Catholic bishops. He himself had written five volumes on Charles Borromeo, a bishop greatly associated with the Council of Trent. See A. Roncalli, *Gli Atti della visita apostolica di s. Carlo Borromeo a Bergamo*. Florence, 1936–1957.

31. See Hans Urns von Balthasar, *The Office of Peter and the Structure of the Church*, San Francisco: Ignatius, 1986.

32. The Decree Concerning the Pastoral Office of Bishops, *Christus Dominus* (28 October 1965), nn. 5 and 36.

33. *Christus Dominus*, nn. 37 and 38

34. 6 August 1966.

35. See *Christus Dominus*, n. 27; the Decree on the Ministry and Life of Priests, *Presbyterorum ordinis* (7 December 1965), n. 7 and the *Motu proprio, Ecclesiae sanctae*, n. 15.

36. See the Catholic Church's *Code of Canon Law*, nn. 515 and 536.

37. See *Christus Dominus*, n. 27.

38. *Apostolicam actuositatem*, n. 26.

39. Cf. also *Christus Dominus*, n. 27 and the Council's Decree on the Missionary Activity of the Church, *Ad gentes* (7 December 1965), n. 30.

40. See *Christus Dominus*, nn. 33–35, *Ecclesiae sanctae*, nn. 22–40.
41. Nn. 13–14.
42. See Hervé-M Legrand, 'Synodes et conciles de l'après-concile: Quelques enjeux ecclésiologiques', *Nouvelle Revue Theéologique* 98 (1976), pp. 193–216.
43. See George Tavard, 'The Catholic Church as Conciliar Church', *Priests and People* (2000/1), pp. 3–7.
44. See Sergei Hackel, 'Sobornost' in Nicholas Lossky et al. (eds), *Dictionary of the Ecumenical Movement*, Geneva: WCC, 2002, pp. 1042–1044.
45. *Church, World, Mission,* Christwood, NY: St Vladimir's Press, 1979, p. 164.
46. See further, Susan Woods, 'Ecclesial Koinonia in Ecumenical Dialogues', *One in Christ* 30 (1994), pp. 124–145.
47. See World Council of Churches, Faith and Order Paper, n. 59, 'Conciliarity and the Future of the Ecumenical Movement', Faith and Order: Louvain, 1971: *Study Reports and Documents*, Geneva: 1971, pp. 225–229, here, p. 226.
48. 'Conciliarity and the Future of the Ecumenical Movement', n. 3 at p. 226.
49. 'Conciliarity and the Future of the Ecumenical Movement', n. 11, pp. 229–230.
50. Group des Dombes, *Un Seul Maitre (Mt 23:8): L'autorité Doctrinale dans l'Église*, Paris: Bayard, 2005, nn. 455–463 at pp. 209–215.
51. *Un Seul Maitre*, n. 457 at p. 212.
52. See S. Dianich, 'Sinodalità', op. cit., p. 1526.
53. *Novo millennio Ineunte*, n. 15.
54. See *Un Seul Maitre*, n. 425 at p. 197.
55. See Walter Kasper, *Theology and Church* (London: SCM, 1989), p. 153.
56. Ratzinger, 'The Ecclesiology', pp. 131–132.
57. *Novo millennio Ineunte*, n. 43.
58. K. Rahner, 'Spirituality of the Future' in Karl Rahner, *The Practice of Faith*, London: SCM, 1985, pp. 18–26, p. 25.
59. Paul VI, Apostolic Exhortation, *Evangelii Nuntiand*, 8 December 1975, n. 41.

60. See Medhard Kehl, *La Chiesa*, Milan: San Paolo, 1995, pp. 219–224; M. de C. Azevedo, *Basic Ecclesial Communities in Brazil: The Challenge of a New Way of Being Church*, Washington: Georgetown University, 1987.

61. See Kehl, *La Chiesa*, pp. 225–226. B. Ugeux, *Les petites communautés chrétiennes, una alternative aux paroisses? L'expérience du Zaïr*, Paris, 1988.

62. Kehl, *La Chiesa*, pp. 226–231.

63. See Address of Pope John Paul II on the occasion of the Meeting with the Ecclesial Movements and New Communities, Rome, 30 May 1998 in Pontifical Council for the Laity, *Movements in the Church*, Vatican, 1999, pp. 221–223.

64. Cf. *Novo millennio Ineunte*, n. 25. See *Lumen gentium*, n. 8 and *Ad gentes*, n. 5.

65. Cf. *Novo millennio Ineunte*, n. 29.

66. *Paul's Prison Letters*, New York: New City, 1997, p. 46.

67. See I. De la Potterie, *The Hour of Jesus,* Alba House, Staten Island, New York, 1989.

The Cornerstones of
Liturgical Renewal:
Sacrosanctum concilium

Susan K. Roll

Among all the changes in the Church laid at the feet of
Vatican II, what do you think particularly older people in a
parish would name as the most significant change in the
Church? Quite likely they would name changes in the
liturgy or, more specifically, the use of the vernacular
language in the liturgy. And, if they were being honest,
almost all of these people and a majority of priests active in
ministry in the 1960s would have testified to a strong sense
of disorientation – that they did not know what had hit
them.

Most priests had received little or no preparation in the
seminary for what was to come. In the past decade I have
made a habit of asking priest colleagues ordained before
1965 how much they had known in advance of the issues
under discussion and new thinking regarding the liturgy
that were to be embodied in foundational Church law at
Vatican II. Only occasionally do I hear that their liturgy
professor in seminary gave them a sense of which potential
changes were under discussion. Once I heard, 'We
seminarians didn't hear anything in class, but we were
reading journals such as *Worship* for ourselves and in our

spare moments we would educate each other'. Most of them reply, 'I didn't know much at all in 1963, we had never discussed these issues in my seminary classes in liturgy and rubrics'. And not infrequently I hear, 'Our seminary liturgy professor was up to date on the issues but he was afraid to discuss them in our classes due to possible reprisals. It was simply too dangerous'. And if the clergy were by and large unprepared, the people in the pews were even less prepared to understand the radical overhaul of liturgical theology that underlay the liturgical revisions that followed upon the promulgation of *Sacrosanctum concilium*, the Constitution on the Sacred Liturgy, in 1963.

Most theology students and Churchgoers do not realise that the way to Vatican II was in fact prepared by a long development – some date it 75 years before Vatican II, others up to 125 years – by what is known as the Liturgical Movement. Churchgoers in the 1930s and 1940s might have heard of a few forward-thinking experiments carried out, here and there, but generally very few folks in the parish could have seen it coming. Many priests and catechists did not see it coming. They may have assumed that the liturgical changes were dreamt up by a few bishops relaxing at a cafe on the Piazza Navona in between Council sessions. This is why it is important to tell something of the story of how we got to Vatican II whenever possible.

So we will sketch the main developments in the Liturgical Movement from its origins on the Continent, with a nod to its spread across the Atlantic, and cite the five main areas in which the movement shifted thinking on the nature and practice of Catholic public worship – the cornerstones of the liturgical reform. Then we will sum up the most significant changes in thought and practice embedded in *Sacrosanctum concilium* that served as foundation stones for the formal liturgical renewal following Vatican II.

The Liturgical Movement[1]

The Liturgical Movement developed across national borders and over several generations. It evolved in roughly three stages: from its original stated purpose of educating clergy and laity in the theology and spirituality of the liturgy as it was in the early twentieth century, towards new thinking about the rites themselves based on research into the ancient Church's worship and finally to advocacy for reform of the rites and a broader re-visioning of liturgical-pastoral theology.

By the early nineteenth century the Catholic Church across Europe, most particularly in France, had suffered violent reverses in the aftermath of the French Revolution and its political and social consequences. Not only had there been a violent reaction against the poverty and social oppression of the lower classes, but against the institutional Church's alliance with the aristocracy and ruling classes. The Revolution directed peoples' pent-up fury against anything connected with the Church: monasteries were razed, Church property confiscated by the state, religious orders disbanded, priests hounded and eventually forced by law to marry. The eighteenth century Enlightenment belief in the eventual triumph of cool, clear human reason was irrevocably shattered.

Culturally the movement in art, music and literature known as Romanticism marked a disengagement with cold, practical reason and emphasised subjective human emotion. Romanticism lay beneath a strong nostalgic turn towards the past, particularly the Middle Ages or, more precisely, what they imagined the Middle Ages to have been: a time of social stability anchored by the Church in which all knew their place in a stratified society. After the chaos and terror, and in reaction to the fear of revolution by the masses from below, many among the old aristocracy and the new prosperous factory-owners and investors began to see the Church as a potential stabilising element. A growing impulse to turn outside the boundaries of France for a reference point to guarantee stability resulted in the Ultramontanist movement: literally 'looking over the mountains', i.e. the Alps, towards Rome.

In this spirit new Benedictine monasteries were founded in France, Belgium and western Germany throughout the nineteenth century. One of these, the Abbey of Solesmes, purchased and rebuilt as a Benedictine monastic community in 1832 by Prosper Guéranger, reflected both Ultramontanist and nostalgic-medieval thinking on the liturgy. The monks researched Gregorian chant and restored its use in their regular prayer of the Liturgy of the Hours. They promoted the Roman Tridentine liturgy as the norm in all French Churches, which led eventually to the suppression of a rich variety of local neo-Gallican liturgies (regrettably, from most liturgists' perspective). Abbot Guéranger's regular lectures to his monks amounted to systematic liturgical catechesis to help them draw spiritual nourishment from the liturgy. While Guéranger cannot be considered a pioneer in the movement he did recognise the importance of liturgical catechesis (albeit for a small in-house group) as well as the promotion of research into the liturgical texts and sources of the early Church with a view to restoring what was found to be of value.

This turned out to be the start of a movement. These new Benedictine monasteries with their neo-Gothic cloisters – Beuron and Maria Laach in Germany, Maredsous and Keizersberg/Mont César in Belgium – became centres of a growing appreciation for the beauty and spiritual depth of liturgy. They became research centres to develop and use new text-critical methodology (pioneered by Scripture scholars in Germany) to study ancient texts relating to worship in the early Church, thus greatly increasing knowledge available to us on how the ancient Christians actually worshipped, what had disappeared and what was added from age to age, and how much of value had been lost, misunderstood or underrated. Ironically, although the restoration of monastic life arose from the hope of stabilising society, the life of faith and the economic structure in Western Europe, these monasteries became the 'think tanks' for new, almost revolutionary ideas in liturgy – what it was and what had been the peoples' participation in the liturgy in the early Church – and, by extension, what it could mean now.

Several monasteries owned or had access to printing presses and distribution networks for printed materials. Maredsous, for example, had not only been founded by a wealthy publishing family, the Desclée family, but the monks had knowledge and access to the technology for printing books such as catechetical texts. In the early 1880s the first *bilingual missals* in a small pocket-size format were printed by monastery printing presses: Latin in one column, the vernacular language in the next – for lay people, so that they could follow along with the Mass instead of being left on their own to say the Rosary or otherwise occupy themselves in private devotion.

This testified to the beginning of an awareness that the liturgy could nourish the spiritual life of the laity, once they understood more clearly what was going on and could pay attention. The interesting historic irony is that at that moment technically it was *prohibited* under Church law both to translate the texts of the Mass from Latin into any other language and to place the texts of the Mass in the hands of lay people. In 1877 in response to a request from American bishops the Vatican ruled that, by way of exception, a vernacular missal could be produced for the laity only with the local bishop's approval. But since the Council of Trent, vernacular missals had been de facto placed on the Index of Forbidden Books and were only quietly removed in 1897.

Nonetheless such small popular missals grew in popularity and gave evidence of a slowly changing attitude towards the role of the people at Mass. In 1903 in an apostolic letter on Church music, *Tra le sollecitudini*, Pope Pius X, the great champion of frequent communion, praised the 'active participation' of the people in the liturgy. He did not mean what we might assume from our experience. One level of 'active participation' meant encouragement to learn some simple Gregorian chants, in line with Pius' great interest in promoting Gregorian chant, in the line of Guéranger several generations later. Another meaning of 'active participation' at this time was simply the laity's attentive presence and awareness of what was happening in the sanctuary.

A key figure in the next stage of evolution of the liturgical movement was Lambert Beauduin, a monk of the abbey of Keizersberg/Mont-César in Louvain. Formerly a diocesan priest, Beauduin had been involved with a group of priests called the 'Chaplains of Labour' and its outreach to impoverished factory workers. Visualise all the evils you have read about the Industrial Revolution and its effects on displaced factory workers uprooted from the land and crowded into tenements in the cities: large families crowded into poor housing, severely impoverished, often illiterate and under pressure to send children to work in dangerous, noisy factories from an early age to support the family. Beauduin and his co-workers were vividly aware that the working class was becoming increasingly alienated from the Church, a fact of which the bishops and higher clergy who belonged to the upper-middle class and the aristocracy were steadfastly ignorant. Moreover now the working class finally had access to a source of hope for dignity, optimism, a healthier life and a better future for their children – Marxism. When Beauduin entered the newly founded monastery at Louvain and added a monastic spiritual depth to his social consciousness, he saw the spiritual richness of the liturgy as one way in which the ordinary people could obtain support, comfort and hope from the Church.

In 1909 in an address to a catechetical congress at Malines, Beauduin used the phrase which had been introduced by Pius X in *Tra le sollecitudini* in 1903: 'active participation' of the people in the liturgy. Pius had called active participation the primary source of the 'true Christian spirit'. But Beauduin went farther and forcefully made the point that the liturgy could be a powerful means of spiritual enrichment for the laity: he called in effect for a 'democratisation of the liturgy', i.e. to make the liturgy belong to the whole people. Beauduin's principal work was *Liturgy the Life of the Church*,[2] arguing that liturgy should shape the theology of the people, not simple devotions. Already we can see the beginnings of a turn, although still in line with the original intent of the Liturgical Movement, to effectively educate both priests and laity about the structure, dynamics and meaning of liturgy in its whole and its parts, so that it would serve as central to the people's spirituality. Guéranger would have said the laity need not participate since the liturgy was a matter reserved to the clergy, but in this age Pope Pius' emphasis on frequent communion and learning a bit of Gregorian chant nudged forward the movement of liturgy to the level of the people.

The following year, 1910, saw several new journals established, such as *Questions Liturgiques/Studies in Liturgy* at Mont-César, to exchange and discuss the results of the research into ancient sources of the liturgy and contemporary pastoral problems. At seminaries in which students had formerly only studied the technical rubrics of saying Mass properly, courses in the new field of liturgy were set up and remedial study weeks for ordained clergy organised. The chaos and tragedy of World War I in precisely this region (northern France, Belgium and western Germany) put a damper on such projects, but by 1919 they had resumed along with practical experimentation in the liturgy on the parish level. In some German parishes priests began celebrating facing the people or having the people give the responses which had belonged to the servers. The foreseen trickle-down effect from clergy to laity began to take hold as families looked for ways to teach their children what was going on in the liturgy and why, and celebrated the various feasts of the liturgical year in the home.

Beauduin in turn was a powerful influence on the monk who would carry over the Liturgical Movement to the US, Virgil Michel. A monk of St John's Abbey, Collegeville Minnesota, Michel had also been involved in social justice apostolates, had some connections with the Catholic Worker movement and Dorothy Day, and in the 1930s did pastoral work with Native Americans. In 1924 Michel went to Europe, visited Beauduin, then teaching at the Pontifical Institute San Anselmo in Rome, and came home very excited about the new insight that liturgy could be a source of spiritual value. He came back to Collegeville full of energy and enthusiasm about the possibilities for new ways of thinking and celebrating liturgy, and organised the same sort of projects he had seen flourishing in Europe.

These projects, already fairly well developed in the 1920s, include five directions we can identify as the cornerstones of the liturgical renewal to come. They include:

1. Publishing There had already been a German translation of the missal along with French in the 1880s, but by 1910 Mont-César began to publish a people's missalette in monthly installments in French. In 1910 the monks started two regular periodical journals devoted to articles on different aspects of liturgy, directed at the clergy to deepen their awareness. Both journals still exist today, *Tijdschrift voor Liturgie* in Dutch (more pastoral) and *Questions Liturgiques/Studies in Liturgy* bilingual in French/English (more academic). All this was interrupted by World War I and re-started in 1919.

Virgil Michel started the Liturgical Press, still today a major player in English-language publishing on liturgical and scripture topics, modelled on the publishing he saw at Maredsous and Keizersberg Abbeys. He founded the journal *Orate Fratres*, now known as *Worship*, to disseminate information to deepen the clergy's (and by extension the people's) knowledge of and appreciation for the liturgy. The American version of the Liturgical Movement emphasised a link (occasionally an uneasy one) between liturgy and social reform in the wake of the Depression, and thus tended to be more oriented to pastoral work and less to scholarly research. After Michel's death in 1939, liturgical weeks and study conferences were organised every year from 1940 to 1969 in different cities in Canada and the US, first under the auspices of Collegeville, then the Liturgical Conference.

2. Research into the ancient sources on liturgical texts and descriptions. The first liturgy scholars were monks like Bernard Botte of Mont-César, who retrained themselves from other branches of study such as Scripture. The text-critical methodology of Scripture study and comparative religions methodology was similar in approach and had led to Comparative Liturgy as a field of study that began from empirical ritual data linked to theology. One of the first documents translated and made available in a reliable critical edition for scholars was the *Apostolic Tradition of Hippolytus*[3], which, once it became available for study, was used as the pattern for the restored RCIA. The *Didache* and the diary of *Egeria* were discovered, translated and published as critical editions and mined for historical information on liturgy. Such documents showed how liturgical forms had accumulated now-meaningless underbrush from pastoral adaptations to times and culture long past, starting from the early medieval period.

This painstaking research into the worship of the ancient Church led to exciting new theological thinking about Christian worship by the 1920s. One of the major figures, though not uncontroversial, was *Odo Casel* (+1948), a monk of Maria-Laach and chaplain to women monks at Herstelle. Casel based this theology partly on what he (thought he) knew about ancient Greek mystery cults in which the solemn rites made the god and the god's saving deeds present again, and as a result the person overcomes damnation by becoming united with the saving mystery. Casel almost accidentally recovered the real deeper meaning of *zikkaron/anamnesis/memoria* in the meaning of the Christian Eucharist: in the Eucharist Christ's saving action of death and resurrection becomes real, actualised and accessible for all believers (which of course presumes active participation of worshippers in the rites). This was called the *mystery/presence* school of thought concerning the Eucharist, and marked a radical departure from the Enlightenment-era *'ex opere operato'* idea that performing the rite with technical perfection, according to the law, mechanically produces grace as if by magic.

This shift was in line with the increasing awareness of how liturgy might act dynamically in the present to transform believers spiritually, not merely re-present an event in the distant past. Most importantly it shifted the focus of Eucharist from static focus on the presence of Christ in the objects of bread and wine, to the whole integrated dynamic of the Eucharistic action: text, gestures, responses by all, and reception of communion by the laity. Unfortunately Casel could not explain exactly how all this comes about, the mysterious living presence of Christ in the liturgy: it remained on the level of an obscure theory derived from pagan sources. It left little space for the Word of God, and presumed a transcendent, totally-Other God, so another level of evolution would have to take place to relate this ineffable, mysterious liturgy to real life.

3. Improved liturgy courses in seminaries In the early 1900s there were no courses in 'liturgy' in seminaries or universities, and for many Churchmen 'liturgist' was a term of suspicion – too modern, too radical. Seminaries as we said required a 'rubrics' course in the final year to train future priests in the mechanics of how to perform the Mass correctly. Professors in other academic areas had to re-tool their knowledge to be able to teach something about the history and theology of liturgical forms.

4. Study weeks were organised as remedial education of clergy in the field and eventually to meet a growing interest by educated laity such as schoolteachers and catechists in the liturgy. Mont-César started yearly Liturgical Weeks, intensive workshops for clergy, also interrupted by World War I and re-started afterward. The yearly Liturgical Weeks in the US and English-speaking Canada became a serious think-tank on liturgy, attracting thousands of participants, including numbers of lay persons and women religious, many of whom were teaching Gregorian chant to children in the Catholic schools by the 1930s.

5. Pastoral experimentation in parishes after World War I played a very important but often underrated role. For example in 1921, a first experiment took place at the abbey of Maria-Laach when the priest turned to face the people and give them the next response in Latin, so people could repeat the response thus taking the role previously reserved to the servers. New parish architecture experimented with seating in a semi-circle. Individual parish priests in Germany and North America started face-to-face confession with teenagers and in the youth worker movements.

The end of World War II brought a turn in the focus of the Liturgical Movement. During the war the Vatican had attempted to suppress some pastoral experimentation in Germany, and was pacified with a flurry of diplomatic activity. Eventually Rome gave permission to continue with masses in which songs in German linked to different parts of the Mass would be sung by the people. Possibly pastoral liturgy took on more importance because of the severe restrictions on Church activities imposed by the National Socialist government. War led to the need for community by a beleaguered Church.

In a second flurry of energy following the war, the annual study weeks in Europe, Canada and the United States under the auspices of the Liturgical Conference brought together enormous energy and enthusiasm as well as a growing concern with the link between liturgy and social justice. The movement developed somewhat differently in Canada, where much of the new thinking was in evidence at the level of university centres for liturgical music and in movements such as the *Jeunesse Ouvrière Chretienne*, the francophone young workers' movement, but less in parishes as in Europe before and after the war, and to some extent in the US.

Several Vatican documents and reforms paved the way for the new thinking to be embodied in practical reform in the 1960s. Among these were the 1943 encyclical *Mystici Corporis,* which promulgated the idea of the Church, the People of God, as the mystical Body of Christ (a controverted and very suspect theological position in the 1920s precisely because it seemed to imply a democratisation and consequent disempowerment of the hierarchy).

In 1947, the papal encyclical *Mediator Dei* praised the Liturgical Movement and gave it a boost in official credibility, though this was not unqualified praise. *Mediator Dei* promoted 'active participation' of the laity in the liturgy although within a clerical concept of liturgy: that liturgy belonged to the clergy while the laity could participate only within set parameters. In a certain sense the laity now moved from passive dependency to active dependency. The encyclical accepted the model of Christ's mysterious presence in the Eucharistic celebration, though it refused to credit Casel or other 'newer authors', claiming the concept of Christ's living presence derived from scholastic theology.

Mediator Dei also promoted scholarly research into the early Church documentation on liturgy, consistent with the 1943 *Divine Afflante Spirito,* which opened up Catholic biblical scholarship and in effect began to catch up with Protestant research methodology and knowledge. One result of this was to increase appreciation for the Word of God in liturgy. It also shifted the genre of preaching from moralistic homilies to exegetical and practical applications of the message of Scripture: from 'Don't do this' to 'Christ did this for us'.

In this period too, new Liturgical Institutes were founded in Paris, Trier and Notre Dame, Indiana, for further research and to train liturgy scholars at a doctoral level. Now the overall emphasis began to shift from *education* about the liturgy to *reform* of the liturgy in line with the new discoveries in research and the new pastoral needs of a very different world. In a clear shift towards activism, the Movement's leaders began to call openly for certain modest reforms of the liturgy such as the restoration of the Easter Vigil to its proper time of celebration – Saturday night.

The 1950s saw first pastoral experiments with a restored catechumenal process for unbaptised adults in West Africa and France, ironically – two areas in which potential Christians found no support in the local culture. A series of studies and dissertations made clear that with flexibility the ancient model of initiation could be applied to adult Christian initiation in the twentieth century and, particularly, it went hand in hand with a shift in the emphasis in the theology of baptism from removal of original sin to initiation into the living Body of Christ.

The first worldwide policy-level reforms of the liturgy prior to Vatican II included the 1951 restoration of the Easter Vigil to its rightful time, Holy Saturday night. In 1955 the entire original Holy Week cycle was restored. Both of these were based on the research done in the early Church's liturgy and the growing awareness that this could serve as a touchstone for the authenticity of worship in the modern era, adapted to the needs of a world radically different than that of our ancestors in faith.

Thus the foundational principles underlying the liturgical reforms embodied in the Constitution on the

Sacred Liturgy of Vatican II all had their origin over a long period, and at the grassroots level. *Sacrosanctum concilium* was the first document completed at Vatican Council II, passed almost unanimously in 1963. Interestingly the Congregation for Rites of the Curia attempted a few preemptive strikes when they discovered the Council was going to be dealing with liturgy and not merely issuing a few new anathemas: a new breviary was quickly promulgated in 1961, as was a lightly revised Roman Missal in 1962 to try to thwart reform. The most significant and perduring achievements enacted as foundational liturgical law in *Sacrosanctum concilium* (hereafter, *SC*) include:

- *SC* fostered a new esteem and value for the liturgy. Sunday worship was no longer to be seen merely as a matter of perfunctory, compulsory attendance for Catholics but pastoral, dynamic and engaging in nature, the foundation of the entire Christian life. *SC* calls the liturgy the 'summit and source' of the Christian life (§10), an amazing statement when one considers the pastoral reality of the Tridentine mass with its relative distanciation and alienation from the people.

- The central theme of 'active participation' of the people of God runs through the entire document. This strengthened esteem for the role of the assembly was rooted in a renewed theology of baptism. In baptism a Christian dies and rises again with Christ, becoming a new creation and putting on the image of Christ. In the worshipping assembly all participants reflect the living face of Christ to each other, as best they can as flawed human beings. This people of God, a theme developed in subsequent documents of the Council, finds its warrant in I Peter: the people are a royal priesthood with an unalienable dignity of their own rooted in their baptism.

- *SC* supported and promoted scholarly liturgical work. It also reiterated the need for thorough liturgy courses to be offered in seminaries by professors preferably trained at the specialised institutes.

- Various specific elements of renewal included:
  - A greatly enriched 'diet' of Scripture read in liturgy. The Bible proclaimed in the language of the people was seen as indispensable and a mode of Christ's living mysterious presence in the worshipping community. As a result the subsequent reform of the Lectionary expanded the yearly cycle of Sunday readings from one to three, with all four Gospels well represented and a wide variety of Old Testament readings correlated with the Gospel of the day.
  - A simplification of rites to their original 'Roman genius', a spirit of sobriety and dignity rather than repetitive ritual elements whose meaning had been lost.
  - The restoration of a number of elements in the Eucharistic liturgy that testify to the baptismal dignity of the celebrating assembly: a homily rooted in scripture and designed to permit people to apply the insights and teachings of the Bible to their own lives today; the bidding prayers or prayer of the faithful, a way in which the priestly people of God exercise their (common) priesthood by making intercession to God for the needs of the world; a greater variety of Eucharistic prayer options to suit different occasions (reconciliation, prayers for various needs) or for children.

- A process of restructuring and simplification of all the major rites, including the Eucharistic celebration, baptism, the liturgy of the hours, the liturgical year and the sanctoral calendar, the anointing of the sick, penance and others. All the rites were streamlined, in a sense, in order to permit the faithful to understand their significance clearly.
- Adaptation of the various rites to different human cultures. This included greater openness to the use of the vernacular language, which almost inadvertently became the defining liturgical change of Vatican II, rather like a water pipe with a crack that finally bursts. SC expresses openness to a wider variety of local musical styles, though with pride of place still given to the pipe organ. The national conferences of Catholic bishops were to play a pivotal role in proposing adaptations suited to the particular needs of their own people for Vatican approval to be promulgated as local liturgical law.

The entire scope of this reform effort, one which to this day has not been fully realised in its vision, expands and fills out the original meaning of the word 'liturgy' as 'a work of the people': one can read 'of' as, 'by', 'for' or 'on behalf of'.

Liturgy is to remain no longer solely a work *for* or *on behalf of* the people, but also *by the people*. While much remains to be done, such as a rediscovery of the ethical dimension of liturgy rooted in the social justice awareness characteristic of the Liturgical Movement, and a number of issues still need to be addressed, such as an increasing clericalisation of the liturgy and attempts to 'reform the reform' by reinterpreting the intentions of the framers of SC in such a way as to inhibit inculturation and inclusivity of the liturgy, amazing progress has been made in a very short time. The priests and catechists of the 1960s would have every right to be amazed.

Notes

1. Some helpful sources for further reading include Bernard Botte's autobiography, *From Silence to Participation,* Washington DC: Pastoral Press, 1988, originally *Le mouvement liturgique: Témoignages et souvenirs*; the Sacerdotal Communities of St-Severin of Paris and St-Joseph of Nice, *The Liturgical Movement,* New York: Hawthorn Books, 1964, originally *Le renouveau liturgique*; Kathleen Hughes (ed.), *How Firm a Foundation: Voices of the Liturgical Movement,* Collegeville: Liturgical Press, 1990; Robert L. Tudzik (ed.), *How Firm a Foundation: Leaders of the Liturgical Movement,* Collegeville: Liturgical Press, 1990; Keith F. Pecklers, *The Unread Vision: The Liturgical Movement in the United States of America 1926–1955,* Collegeville: Liturgical Press, 1988, especially Chapter One; and James F. White, *Roman Catholic Worship: Trent to Today,* Mahwah: Paulist Press, 1995, especially Chapters 4, 5 and 6.

2. Lambert Beauduin, *Liturgy and the Life of the Church,* trans. Virgil Michel, Collegeville: Liturgical Press, 1929, the English translation of his *La piete liturgique: principes et faits,* Louvain: Bureau des oeuvres liturgiques, 1914.

3. The most often consulted edition was that of Bernard Botte, *La Tradition Apostoloque/Hippolyte de Rome,* Sources chretiennes 11, Paris: Cerf, 1946, although that of Gregory Dix, Apostolic Tradition, London: SPCK, 1934 preceded it by over a decade. The most recent critical commentary is that of Paul Bradshaw, *The Apostolic Tradition: A Commentary,* ed. Paul Bradshaw, Maxwell Johnson and L. Edward Phillips, Minneapolis: Fortress Press, 2002.

Dei verbum
Forty Years Later

Jan Lambrecht SJ

Let me begin this conference on '*Dei verbum* – Forty Years Later' with two personal recollections.

Vatican II and *Dei verbum*

The four sessions of the Second Vatican Council took place from 1962 to 1965, each time in the last months of the year. During that time I happened to be at the Pontifical Biblical Institute in Rome, as a student, a somewhat late vocation for biblical studies. It was a memorable time, not so much because of the troubles at the Biblicum – Father Lyonnet and Father Zerwick were not allowed to teach anymore and this lasted for two or three years – but much more because of the Council itself.

In the first session in November 1962 more than 60 per cent of the Council Fathers voted against the first schema on the two sources of revelation, *De fontibus Revelationis*,[1] as a basis for further discussion. Pope John withdrew that schema and ordered the composition of a new schema by a modified and greatly enlarged commission, the so-called Mixed Commission, chaired by Card. Ottaviani and Card. Bea together. I remember vividly the behind-the-scenes activity of some professors of the Biblicum. Let me just mention the contacts of my promotor and fellow-countryman, Father Ignace de la Potterie[2] with the Belgian College, especially with the bishop of Bruges, Mgr. De Smedt, from the Secretariat on Christian Unity.[3]

In November 1965, after three years of heated discussion but also some periods of unexplained stalemate, the dogmatic Constitution on Divine Revelation *Dei verbum* was promulgated by Paul VI. That is forty years ago.

The 1993 Document: 'The Interpretation of the Bible in the Church'

In the early 1990s, as one of the twenty members of the international Pontifical Biblical Commission, I could modestly help prepare the text that became known as 'The Interpretation of the Bible in the Church' and, according to the explicit wishes of Pope John Paul II, was published in 1993. That teamwork was not easy: the first concept, the division of the work, the individual homework – that is the writing of a personal paper on a theme or a section of the draft – and back in Rome the patient and laborious discussion of these papers in the group together, then the slow redaction of the final draft and, at the end, the voting on paragraph after paragraph with the possibility of a *placet iuxta modum*.

During this lengthy process most of us were of the opinion that actually we were preparing the materials for a new encyclical, one hundred years after *Providentissimus Deus* of 1893 and fifty years after *Divino afflante Spiritu* of 1943. But then suddenly it was announced that the Commission should publish the document under its own name. The day of publication, however, was meant to be solemn. In April of 1993, during the course of a special audience, commemorating that centenary and that fiftieth anniversary, Pope John Paul delivered an address. The Pope praised the document's openness, its balance and moderation. The document examines the methods, approaches and interpretations that are practised in exegesis today. In almost every case, before some critical observations, the presence of valid elements for an integral interpretation of the biblical text are duly acknowledged. One can say that generally the document 'The Interpretation of the Bible in the Church' has been well received by Catholics and many non-Catholics alike. The Biblical Commission wanted to remain faithful to the spirit and openness of *Dei verbum*.[4]

A Brief Analysis of *Dei verbum*
Returning to *Dei verbum* itself, the 'Dogmatic Constitution on Divine Revelation': what was its importance in 1965 and what is its significance in 2005, forty years later?

In the major German commentary on the documents of Vatican II, published in German in 1968, Joseph Ratzinger is the main author on *Dei verbum*.[5] According to Ratzinger three motifs came together so that the need was felt for a Constitution on Revelation: first, the ongoing reflection on tradition (cf. Adam Möhler, Henri Newman, Maurice Blondel);[6] second, the application of the critical historical methods in the interpretation of Scripture; third, the ever-increasing biblical movement, also in Catholic circles, to which the ecumenical climate of those days may be added.

For an evaluation of the document several data must be taken into account:

1. One should realise that *Dei verbum* is not exclusively biblical, as becomes evident from the title itself – 'Dogmatic Constitution on Divine Revelation'. The

101

twenty-six numbers of the document are divided into six chapters: (1) Divine Revelation Itself; (2) The Transmission of Divine Revelation; (3) Sacred Scripture: Its Divine Inspiration and its Interpretation; (4) The Old Testament; (5) The New Testament; and (6) Sacred Scripture in the Life of the Church. So there can be no doubt, *Dei verbum* deals with oral tradition and written texts, with Tradition and Scripture.

2. The new draft of 1963 was in fact meant as a compromise text.[7] The new schema had been prepared by the Mixed Commission – consisting of the old Theological Commission, of members of the Secretariat for Christian unity and augmented by some Cardinals and a number of more or less well-known *periti*. It had been sent out to the Fathers in the middle of 1963 for evaluation. The written comments by the Council Fathers were then discussed by that Commission and integrated into a rewritten text that was put to a vote within the Mixed Commission itself in June 1964. A consensus, however, could not be reached, so that at the beginning of the third session in 1964 both the majority (called progressive, 17) and the minority (called conservative or 'traditionalists', 7) had their report (*relatio*) read.

The main point of disagreement was the relation between Scripture and Tradition, between 'written books and unwritten traditions' (Trent).[8] Does divine apostolic Tradition contain quantitatively more revelation, more revealed truths than Scripture alone? According to the majority, the rewritten text of the new schema does not want to answer this question: the schema does not intend to present '*Traditionem velut quantitativum S. Scripturae supplementum*' nor '*Scripturam velut integrae revelationis codificationem*' (from the majority report of archbishop Florit). Theologians must further reflect on this matter; the debate is not closed. The minority, however, with a number of reasons and references to older documents, argued that an answer must be provided: according to this position the Tradition possesses a greater objective content than Scripture does.[9]

3. In order to understand the way Tradition is conceived in *Dei verbum* one has to see how revelation itself is presented. Revelation is not just the communication of doctrine; it is much more than an intellectual enterprise. Divine revelation must be appropriately responded to in faith and trust, i.e. by the whole human person. One becomes personally involved. God reveals himself in Jesus Christ. As the self-manifestation of God in Christ, revelation is theocentric as well as Christocentric. Jesus Christ manifested God through his whole life on earth; revelation is not only a matter of words, but also of revelatory deeds and significant gestures; works and words belong together. Therefore, both Scripture and Tradition are not viewed 'statistically, as depositories containing particular truths, but rather dynamically, as ways in which God converses with his People (*DV* 8 and 21). Scripture itself is actively handed down ... in the Church. Tradition, moreover, consists not simply in oral and written statements but in the total life and practice of the praying and believing Church'.[10]

Tradition and Scripture belong together. We may quote *Dei verbum* itself:

Sacred Tradition and Sacred Scripture ... are bound together, and communicate one with the other. For both of them, flowing out from the same divine well-spring, come together in some fashion to form one thing, and move towards the same goal. Sacred Scripture is the speech of God as it is put down in writing under the breath of the Holy Spirit. And Tradition transmits in its entirety the Word of God which has been entrusted to the apostles by Christ the Lord and the Holy Spirit. Tradition transmits it to the successors of the apostles ... Thus it comes about that the Church does not draw her certainty about all revealed truths from the holy Scriptures alone ... (DV 9)

Tradition thus is likewise a form of the Word of God.

4. But while listening to this last text we again feel confronted with the problem of what precisely Tradition reveals more than Scripture. Of course due distinction must be made between divine apostolic Tradition (spelled with capital T and in the singular) and the most diverse later traditions (creeds, dogmas, liturgy and the like).[11] All of us have to accept at least that through Tradition we acknowledge the binding authority, the canon of Scripture. Moreover, there is evidently a prior oral tradition of which Holy Scripture is a privileged sedimentation. Furthermore, Scripture is read in the light of an ongoing tradition assisted by the living Spirit. One cannot bypass tradition.[12]

Dulles expounds: 'In the early centuries it may have been possible to identify certain particular traditions as coming from the apostles by word of mouth. Theologians speculate that doctrines such as infant baptism and the perpetual virginity of Mary may have been transmitted in this way. But at the distance of many centuries scientific history can no longer establish the apostolic origin of these doctrines. Thus the concept of tradition as a source of factual information, parallel with and alongside of Holy Scripture, has been losing favor'.[13] Perhaps one could put forward that all revealed truth is in some way contained in Scripture, but that Tradition is needed to grasp it with the required assurance.

5. From chapter III to the very end, chapter VI (i.e. numbers 11–26), attention is directed to Sacred Scripture itself. Much is repeated, both as to spirit and content, of what can already be found in *Divino afflante Spiritu* of 1943. One can equally compare this Constitution with the then recent but important *Instructio de historica Evangeliorum veritate* of the Papal Biblical Commission (*Sancta Mater Ecclesia*, April 1964). Among the to-be-expected items in *Dei verbum* are:

- The inspiration;
- The history of salvation (*oeconomia salutis*);
- Old and New Testament and their mutual dependence (according the famous words of St Augustine: '*Novum in Vetere latet et in Novo Vetus patet*');
- The historicity of the Bible, at least *nostrae salutis causa*: 'we must acknowledge that the books of Scripture, firmly, faithfully and without error, teach that truth which God, *for the sake of our salvation*, wished to see confided to the Sacred Scripture';[14]
- The correct interpretation of Scripture;
- The presence in Scripture of '*genera litteraria*' (modes of speech, literary forms);
- The growth of understanding (a deeper '*perceptio*'; a progressive penetration of the meaning);
- The task and authority of the magisterium: 'Yet this

Magisterium is not superior to the Word of God, but is its servant';[15]
- The need of translations;
- The use of Scripture in theology, in liturgy;
- Catechesis and spirituality.

6. In his commentary, A. Grillmeier writes: 'During the preparatory period and in the first sessions of the Council mistrust had become evident against the more modern-minded exegetes. For this reason it was not easy to get the fathers to say a good word for the representatives of scriptural studies.'[16] Yet in *Dei verbum* the work of the exegetes is now highly respected; it is needed for the deepening and clarification of insight; it assists the teaching authority: *'ut, quasi praeparato studio, iudicium Ecclesiae maturetur'* (*DV* 12). One reads near the end of *Dei verbum*: the Council 'encourages those sons of the Church who are engaged in biblical studies constantly to renew their efforts, in order to carry on the work they have so happily begun with complete dedication and in accordance with the mind of the Church' (*DV* 23).[17]

Critical Observations
Because of its open and theologically rich qualities the dogmatic Constitution on Revelation has been received very positively. Yet, what kind of less positive impressions are left after a new reading, now forty years later? I endeavour to mention five of them:

1. A number of affirmations in the document may strike many readers today as being sorely in need of qualification. Does *Dei verbum* really follow in the steps of Trent and Vatican I as is stated in *DV* 1?[18] *DV* 4 ends

as follows in a (too?) confident manner: 'The Christian economy ... since it is the new and definitive covenant, will never pass away; and no new public revelation is to be expected before the glorious manifestation of our Lord, Jesus Christ'. In *DV* 10 it is stated in a quite peremptory and exclusive way: 'The task of giving an authentic interpretation of the Word of God ... has been entrusted to the living teaching office of the Church alone'. In chapter 11 *DV* asserts: 'it was as true authors that they – the men chosen by God – consigned to writing whatever he [God] wanted written, and no more'. Is the tone in all this not too self-certain?[19]

2. God's plan, his *oeconomia salutis,* is depicted as if it were all but evident to humans. One would, of course, not like to criticise the end of *DV* 2: 'The most intimate truth which this revelation gives us about God and the salvation of man shines forth in Christ, who is himself both the mediator and the sum total of Revelation'. But what about *DV* 3: 'After the fall ... [God] never ceased to take care of the human race'? This may be true, but do many people really experience that care? And can believers so easily accept that 'the economy of the Old Testament was deliberately so orientated that it should prepare for and declare in prophecy the coming of Christ, redeemer of all men, and of the messianic kingdom' (*DV* 15)?

3. In *Dei verbum* there is, it would seem, too much systematisation, perhaps even simplification. There is in many instances a tension between abstract affirmation and concrete, often difficult and confusing biblical texts. In actual world history there seems to be much lack of purpose and there remains much more obscurity than

the Council Fathers appear to assume. Salvation history does not appear to be so linear as *DV* 7 depicts it (from Christ to the Apostles to their successors, i.e. the bishops) or in *DV* 14 (from Abraham through Moses to Israel; the prophets make the ways of God 'more widely known among the nations'). See also *DV* 19 as to the procedure the evangelists used in composing their gospels: 'The sacred authors ... selected certain of the many elements which had been handed on ... others they synthesized or explained with an eye to the situation of the churches ... always in such a fashion that they have told us the honest truth about Jesus'. Was all this in the mind of the authors so conscious and intentional? In chapter 21 not a word is said about the fact that for centuries the Bible remained almost secret and Scripture was kept away from the mass of Catholic believers.[20]

4. Many find in sections of *Dei verbum* a too idealistic, over-optimistic vision that is not completely different from the very 'triumphalism' so severely blamed by some Patres in the aula. Several passages have an attractive, even enthusiastic ring, for example: 'both Scripture and Tradition must be accepted and honored with equal feelings of devotion and reverence' (*DV* 9); or on God's marvellous condescension in Scripture just as in the incarnation: 'Indeed the words of God, expressed in the words of men, are in every way like human language, just as the Word of the eternal Father, when he took on himself the flesh of human weakness, became like men' (*DV* 13); or, again, in comparison with the Eucharist: 'The Church has always venerated the divine Scriptures as she venerated the Body of the Lord, in so far as she never ceases ... to partake of the bread of life and to offer it to the faithful from the one table of the Word of

God and the Body of Christ' (*DV* 21: *'sumere panem vitae ex mensa tam verbi Dei quam Corporis Christi'*). See also in chapter 25 the famous quotation of Saint Jerome: *'Ignoratio enim Scripturarum ignoratio Christi est'*. Nonetheless, there is no mention of the possibility of distorting traditions.[21]

5 Assertive language (a), too easily supposed evidence (b), simplifying systematisation (c) and self-confident, almost triumphalistic description (d) each of the many cited examples of this necessarily brief document can most probably be defended as to its content, or explained. Yet during the last forty years modern Catholicism has become more critical, less confident, more prudent and, rightly so, more discreet. (e) A last point of criticism should not go unnoticed. Taking into account the lengthy process and the manifold reworking and rewriting, as well as the additions and corrections (the *modi*), one should forgive much of the rather heavy style of this Latin document. Yet a composition which brings together such an abundance of scriptural citations and references to the Patres and the Magisterium, especially the recent popes, can hardly be hermeneutically recommendable. By way of example let me refer to the rather brief number 17, which introduces the chapter on the New Testament: in the whole of six Latin sentences there are no less than six references to Scripture: Romans, Galatians, John (three times) and Ephesians with no regard to their respective contexts and literal sense.

Scripture Today
Catholic biblical scholars must be grateful for the Constitution *Dei verbum* of Vatican II. Its holistic view of

God's revelation and human acceptance is remarkable. To a large extent it is and remains an open document. It provides Catholic exegetes with freedom in their research. It stresses the function of the Bible in the life of the Church. It encourages scholars in their labour. Its spirit is ecumenical. It often accentuates the progress of insight still to be achieved (see *DV* 5, 8, 12, 23). So far, so good.

We will now look at the question of relevance – What is the significance of *Dei verbum* still today?[22] My intention is to point out actual problems for which the solutions are not – or not fully – provided by *Dei verbum*. One can and must look for help in the more recent 'The Interpretation of the Bible in the Church', the 1993 document of the Pontifical Biblical Commission, for we justly appreciate that in this last document, as far as methodology is concerned, the valid solid results of the historical-critical method are duly recognised. A brief reflection is offered on hermeneutics; the literal sense and the spiritual sense are dealt with. Furthermore many paragraphs deal with the place of the Bible in the life of the Church. Ecumenism is praised and encouraged. We may still add one more comment. Catholic scholars today, the document says, can rightly be proud since, finally, they can read and discuss the Bible with their colleagues, separated brothers and sisters, on an equal scientific footing.[23]

What are the main areas of evolution and more deepening insight? And what are the areas of conflict with earlier private or official convictions of forty years ago?

1. A first problem is the so-called crisis regarding the historical-critical method.[24] *Dei verbum* 12 is devoted to the interpretation of the Bible.[25] I quote a few sentences: 'Seeing that, in sacred Scripture, God speaks through men in human fashion, it follows that the interpreter of sacred

Scripture, if he is to ascertain what God has wished to communicate to us, should carefully search out the meaning which the sacred writers really had in mind, that meaning which God had thought well to manifest through the medium of their words'. Then *DV* says that attention must be paid *inter alia* to the literary forms. Of course, Sacred Scripture must also be interpreted with its divine authorship in mind; hence, no less attention must be devoted to the content and unity of the whole of Scripture, taking into account the Tradition of the entire Church and the analogy of faith. Ultimately the manner of interpreting Scripture is subject to the judgement of the teaching authority of the Church.[26] Nonetheless, the beginning of *DV* 12, understood in the line of *Divino afflante Spiritu*, is an encouragement to use scientific research, the historical-critical method.

In January 1988 the Erasmus lecture in New York was delivered by Joseph Cardinal Ratzinger: 'Biblical Interpretation in Crisis: On the Question of the Foundations and Approaches of Exegesis Today'. In his paper, in the press conference and during the subsequent seminar the late Raymond Brown defended historical biblical criticism. Many felt that his positive attitude was to some extent opposed to the warnings and reservations of the Cardinal, who refers to the philosophical presuppositions of Dibelius and Bultmann. Therefore, in the publication of his paper Brown appends *Addenda*, which expand on the convergences and differences between the Cardinal and himself.[27]

In the Introduction of PBC's document 'The Interpretation of the Bible in the Church' of 1993 reference is made to this so-called crisis. I quote:

All those who have acquired a solid formation in this area [i.e. of the modern methods] consider it quite impossible to return to a precritical level of interpretation, a level which they now rightly judge to be quite inadequate.

But the fact is that at the very time when the most prevalent scientific method – the 'historical-critical method' – is freely practised in exegesis, including Catholic exegesis, it is itself *brought into question*. To some extent, this has come about in the scholarly world through the rise of alternative methods and approaches. But it has also arisen through the criticisms of many members of the faithful, who judge the method deficient from the point of view of faith.

The diversity of interpretations only serves to show, they say, that nothing is gained by submitting biblical texts to the demands of scientific method; on the contrary, they allege, much is lost. They insist that the result of scientific exegesis is only to provoke perplexity and doubt upon numerous points that hitherto had been accepted without difficulty. They add that it impels some exegetes to adopt positions contrary to the faith of the Church on matters of great importance, such as the virginal conception of Jesus, his miracles and even his resurrection and divinity.

Even when it does not end up in such negative positions, scientific exegesis, they claim, is notable for its sterility in what concerns progress in the Christian life. Instead of making for easier and more secure access to the living sources of God's Word, it makes of the Bible a closed book. Interpretation may always have been something of a problem, but now it requires such technical refinements as to render it a domain reserved for a few specialists alone (pp. 30–31).

Notwithstanding all these criticisms the historical-critical method is strongly defended by the PBC in its document:[28] 'The historical-critical method is the indispensable method for the scientific study of the meaning of ancient texts' (p. 34). Proper understanding of the Bible 'not only admits the use of this method but actually requires it' (Ibid.). The method 'seeks to shed light upon the historical processes which gave rise to biblical texts, diachronic processes that were often complex and involved a long period of time ... In each of its steps (from textual criticism to redaction criticism) it operates with the help of scientific criteria that seek to be as objective as possible' (p. 37). Of itself it implies no *a priori*. 'If its use is accompanied by *a priori* principles, that is not something pertaining to the method itself, but to certain hermeneutical choices which govern the interpretation and can be tendentious ... The early confrontation between traditional exegesis and the scientific approach, which initially consciously separated itself from faith and at times even opposed it, was assuredly painful; later however it proved to be salutary; once the method was freed from external prejudices, it led to a more precise understanding of the truth of Sacred Scripture' (p. 39).[29]

Many theologians, however, are of the opinion that the use of the historical-critical method is still accompanied by presuppositions that are harmful to religious faith. Moreover, some exegetes, also Catholic scholars, assert that 'the presuppositions of historical criticism and faith assumptions are mutually incompatible, and that exegetes should systematically exclude all propositions based on faith in order to produce a purely critical biblical theology'.[30] Can the method be practised in complete neutrality?[31] Is complete objectivity the ideal? Further, one should not be naive: critical history has sometimes served to undermine faith in traditional Christian doctrine and in the trustworthiness of the Bible. Moreover, a well-known complaint says that the method often remains absorbed in hypothetical reconstructions of the past.[32] The text is often not explained in the context of the book or in that of the canon. The results of the historical-critical method do not constitute a complete exegesis.[33]

2. A second problem concerns the meaning of the sacred text.[34] What is the relation between the literal sense and the more-than-literal, spiritual or theological sense (and also the '*sensus plenior*')? In *Dei verbum* the fathers understand the literal sense as the sense intended by the human author, the authorial sense: the exegete should determine 'the intention of the sacred writers' (n. 12). One easily realises, however, that 'writer' or 'author' in the Bible cannot be understood in a simplistic way.[35]

Moreover, modern hermeneutics[36] pays more attention to the meaning present in the text ('text-centered')[37], as it were no longer bound to its author, and to the active role of the reader in constituting the sense of what they read ('reader-oriented').[38] Yet, the literal sense is the sense the author meant in the past and to grasp it one should take into account the historical circumstances as much as they can be recovered. Furthermore, hermeneutics teaches us that in a certain manner all authors from the past still speak to human beings living in the present: a text still means something for present and future generations. But is that sense still intended by the human author and how can it legitimately be discerned? Again, it is well known that in the Bible later authors re-read former texts (relecture) and, almost inevitably, altered their original meaning to some extent. In its new context a new literal sense is created by the new human author.[39]

Yet the situation of the Bible is even more complex. Its main author is God. That divine authorship is very much emphasised in *Dei verbum*.[40] God speaks through men in human fashion. 'The interpreter should carefully search out the meaning which the sacred writers really had in mind, that meaning which God had thought well to manifest through the medium of their words' (*DV* 12). Peter S. Williamson comments: 'The addition of the latter phrase suggests, first, that the Council Fathers did not simply equate the human author's meaning with the divine intention, and, second, that they did not want to limit the work of exegetes to explaining the human author's intentions in their historical circumstances'.[41]

The *IBC* provides the following definition of the spiritual sense (with the qualification 'as a general rule'): '...the meaning expressed by the biblical texts when read under the influence of the Holy Spirit, in the context of the paschal mystery of Christ and of the new life which flows from it' (p. 81).[42] It is a sense willed by God himself, given by God to the text. This sense is not a subjective interpretation stemming from free imagination or intellectual speculation.[43] According to the *IBC*, 'the spiritual sense can never be stripped of its connection with the literal sense. The latter remains the indispensable foundation. Otherwise, one could not speak of the "fulfilment" of Scripture. Indeed, in order that there be fulfilment, a relationship of continuity and of conformity is essential. But it is also necessary that there be transition to a higher level of reality' (p. 82).

The *IBC* also explains: 'Contrary to a current view, there is not necessarily a distinction between the two senses. When a biblical text relates directly to the paschal mystery of Christ or to the new life which results from it, its literal sense is already a spiritual sense. Such is regularly the case in the New Testament. It follows that it is most often in dealing with the Old Testament that Christian exegesis speaks of the spiritual sense. But already in the Old

Testament, there are many instances where texts have a religious or spiritual sense as their literal sense. Christian faith recognises in such cases an anticipatory relationship to the new life brought by Christ' (p. 82).[44] Dealing with the Old Testament, *Dei verbum* writes: 'These books, even though they contain matters imperfect and provisional, nevertheless show us authentic divine teaching. Christians should accept with veneration these writings which give expression to a lively sense of God, which are a storehouse of sublime teaching on God and of sound wisdom on human life, as well as a wonderful treasury of prayers; in them, too, the mystery of our salvation is present in a hidden way' (n. 15).

'Spiritual interpretation, whether in community or in private, will discover the authentic spiritual sense ... when one holds together three levels of reality: the biblical text, the paschal mystery and the present circumstances of life in the Spirit' (*IBC*, p. 82). In his Preface to the *IBC*, Cardinal Ratzinger asserts that the document 'inquires into how the meaning of scripture might become known – this meaning in which the human word and God's word work together in the singularity of historical events and the eternity of the everlasting Word which is contemporary in every age. The biblical word comes from a real past; it comes not only from the past, however, but at the same time from the eternity of God and it leads us into God's eternity, but again along the way through time, to which the past, the present and the future belong' (pp. 26–27).

Of course, one should keep in mind that the Bible and its senses must not be confused with what is called dogmatic development or the evolution of the doctrine in later Church history. Yet this last remark confronts us again with the unsolved question of content mentioned before: what is the relation between Scripture and Tradition, here more concretely between Scripture and creed and/or later Church doctrine?

3. A third problem is that of historicity and *Sachkritik*, i.e. criticism of the substance itself. The claim that the Bible is a historical book must be further qualified. One could refer here to the painstaking analysis of miracles and prophecies in the Old and New Testament, the so-called external signs of credibility. But let us rather focus on what is occurring nowadays in the confrontation between scholars in view of the new archeological data in Israel. To what extent can the biblical texts on David and Solomon still be called historical? It is no longer the figure or date of Abraham and Moses, the occurrence of the Exodus and the conquest of the promised Land; it is no longer Jericho and its walls, but, for example, the findings in Megiddo that are critically re-examined.[45] A whole stretch of biblical literature that was considered until recently historically trustworthy perhaps no longer appears to be. One cannot but somewhat critically reflect on *DV* 14: 'By his covenant with Abraham ... and, through Moses, with the race of Israel ... he did acquire a people for himself, and to them he revealed himself in words and deeds as the one, true, living God, so that Israel might experience the ways of God with men'.

But there is more. All of us are acquainted with historical criticism, fairly enough. But to what degree has *Sachkritik* become unavoidable today and, therefore, permitted and needed? Let us, for example, admit with good arguments that both Matthew and Luke were convinced of the conception of Jesus by the Holy Spirit, thus of the virginal conception of Mary. But not only unbelieving or protestant exegetes but also good Catholic and exegetically competent scholars[46] ask the radical question: must we and can we still accept such a Matthean and Lukan conviction? Should the coming into existence of this affirmation, namely 'for the child conceived in [Mary] is from the Holy Spirit' (Mt 1:20), not be respectfully explained in a natural, almost self-evident way as a christologoumenon, most probably without a biological basis? More or less similar examples could be brought forward. With this one example one easily realises the upheaval that such an approach already creates and will create among the non-specialist devout Christians, not to mention the difficulties with part of the Magisterium.

4. What about the use of the Bible in the Liturgy? Thirty or thirty-five years after the liturgical reform, one is confronted with the serious problem of the wide division of the readings of the Old Testament and the New Testament (for Sundays and for weekdays). Are a number of these short Scripture passages out of context really understandable? A fundamental question is: Do three so different readings during the same Eucharist not cause indigestion and confusion in the mind of listeners? Do they not equally give rise to artificial combinations in a necessarily too brief homily, notwithstanding the numerous valid both liturgical and homiletical publications? It would seem that after this long period a pastoral evaluation is now needed. Perhaps a new reform is indicated; however, not before serious reflection: What must be done and what can be done?

5. My last problem concerns actualisation.[47] The term is not used in *Dei verbum* and therefore Fitzmyer can state: 'What is new in the 1993 document of the Biblical Commission is the emphasis given to the "actualization" of the literal sense of Scripture'.[48]

The problem can perhaps be introduced as follows. In the 1993 document straightforward language is used against the fundamentalist reading. 'The fundamentalist approach is dangerous, for it is attractive to people who look to the Bible for ready answers to the problems of life. It can deceive these people, offering them interpretations that are pious but illusory, instead of telling them that the Bible does not necessarily contain an immediate answer to each and every problem. Without saying as much in so many words, fundamentalism actually invites people to a kind of intellectual suicide. It injects into life a false certitude, for it unwittingly confuses the divine substance of the biblical message with what are in fact its human limitations' (p. 72).

There has been criticism against this rather harsh language, justified or not justified. But the everyday problem remains: how can modern Christians use the Bible for their concrete life of prayer and action, for inspiration and spirituality? To what extent is it legitimate to find in the psalms and the gospels one's own insights and questions, thus to find in the Bible consolation and strength? Must not a clear distinction be made between responsible official use of the Bible according to strict scientific and ecclesial rules on the one hand and on the other a much more free and devotional yet legitimate use?[49] Is reading the Bible not as it were *ipso facto* 'sacramental', always a grace?[50]

Nevertheless, we members of the Irish Biblical Association believe that also through our work the promise of the Johannine Jesus is being fulfilled in some measure: 'When the Spirit of truth comes, he will guide you into all truth, *in plenitudinem veritatis*' (Jn 16:13; cf. *DV* 5 and 20). [51] Methodological correctness and Church loyalty should not be unduly opposed. And since 'just as the Bible comes from preaching, work on the Bible must lead back to preaching',[52] we hope that somehow through our biblical endeavour of study and research, of teaching and occasional preaching *'mundus universus audiendo credat, credendo speret, speranda amet'*, in translation 'that the whole world through hearing may believe, through belief it may hope, through hope it may come to love' (*DV* 1; with reference to Augustine).

Notes

1. On the background of this first draft (and its defence), see K. Schelkens, 'Lucien Cerfaux and the Preparations of the Schema *De Fontibus Revelationis*', *The Belgian Contribution to the Second Vatican Council. An International Research Conference at Mechelen, Leuven and Louvain-la-Neuve (Sept. 12–16, 2005).*

2. I remember his impassioned struggle for the correct interpretation of the expression *'nostrae salutis causa'* in *DV* 11, which deals with the truth of Scripture: *'causa'* is not a nominative, as in the first translation of the text in the *Osservatore Romano*, but an ablative, and qualifies the historicity of the biblical text: only the truth which God revealed 'for the sake of our salvation'. As you probably know *'veritas'* has been the center of I. de la Potterie's research, truth in the fullness of the scriptural idea, above all the truth of revelation, the self-communication of God, his truthfulness and fidelity, but also the authenticity and transparence of the life of men and women.

3. In his famous intervention on 19 November 1962, Bishop De Smedt pointed out that the Pope had assigned to that Secretariat the task of advising the commissions on ecumenical questions. The Theological Commission, however, had refused to accept this advice. So the influence of the Secretariat on the schemata was invisible: no contribution was made to the ecumenical dialogue. On the two sources the bishop declared publicly in the aula: 'The schema is a step backwards, a hindrance, it does damage'.

4. See The Pontifical Biblical Commission, *The Interpretation of the Bible in the Church*, Rome 1993, with Address of Pope John Paul II, Preface by Cardinal Joseph Ratzinger, Commission's Document (henceforth *IBC*). Cf. J.A. Fitzmyer, *The Biblical Commission's Document* The Interpretation of the Bible in the Church: *Text and Commentary* (Subsidia Biblica, 18), Rome, 1995; P.S. Williamson, *Catholic Principles for Interpreting Scripture: A Study of the Pontifical Biblical Commission's* The Interpretation of the Bible in the Church (Subsidia Biblica, 22), Rome, 2001.

5. For *Dei verbum* see the English translation of this publication: H. Vorgrimler (ed.), *Commentary on the Documents of Vatican II*. Vol. III, New York–London, 1969, pp. 155–272: 'Dogmatic Constitution on Divine Revelation'. The commentary on chapter III is by A. Grillmeier (pp. 199–246), that on Chapters IV and V by B. Rigaux (pp. 247–261). All other sections are by J. Ratzinger. For a succinct bibliograhy on *Dei verbum* see R. Bieringer, 'Biblical Revelation and Exegetical Interpretation According to *Dei verbum* 12', in M. Lamberigts and L. Kenis (eds), *Vatican II and Its Legacy* (BETL 166), Leuven 2002, pp. 26–58 (bibliography on pp. 53–56). On the genesis of the text, see J. Wicks, '*De Revelatione* under Revision 1964: Contributions of Charles Moeller et al.', *The Belgian Contribution* (see note 1).

6. In 1954 the Faith and Order Commission of the World Council of Churches produced a study report *Scripture, Tradition and Traditions*, which was accepted by The Fourth World Conference on Faith and Order in Montreal 1963.

7. Yet see the conclusive statement of Ratzinger, 'Dogmatic Constitution' (n. 5), pp. 164–165: 'But the fundamental compromise which pervades it is more than a compromise, it is a synthesis of great importance ... With regard to its total achievement, one can say unhesitatingly that the labour of the four-year long controversy was not in vain'. Cf. title and content of S. Lyonnet, 'A propos des chapitres IV et VI de la

Dei verbum. L'étonnant chemin parcouru au cours de l'élaboration du texte conciliaire', in R. Latourelle (ed.), *Vatican II. Bilan et perspectives: vingt-cinq ans après (1962–1987)*. Vol. I, Montréal-Paris 1988, pp. 170–221.

8. In the Council of Trent the expression *'partim ... partim'*, that is either in Scripture alone or in tradition alone, had been removed from the final draft. The text of Trent reads as follows: *'in libris scriptis et sine scriptis traditionibus'*.

9. Cf. Ratzinger, 'Dogmatic Consitution' (n. 5), p. 163: during the discussion in the third session 'it became clear that as well as the ... main controversial point there were two further critical points of prime importance: the question of a more detailed account of the "inerrancy" of Scripture and that of the form in which the historicity of the Gospel was to be anchored in the text'.

10. A. Dulles, 'Revelation, Fonts of', in *New Catholic Encyclopedia* (second edition). Vol. 13, p. 192. Cf. T. Merrigan, 'What's in a Word? Revelation and Tradition in Vatican II and in Contemporary Theology', in *Vatican II and Its Legacy* (n. 5), pp. 59–83; Bieringer, 'Biblical Revelation', ibid., pp. 26–27.

11. Cf. Dulles, 'Revelation' (n. 10), p. 192: 'Particular traditions, which may be thought to be apostolic, have to be sifted and evaluated in order to determine their authenticity', and to answer the question, 'how to distinguish genuine tradition from merely human and possibly distorted traditions?', Catholics 'refer to a variety of tests, such as conformity with Scripture, coherence with Catholic tradition as a whole, harmony with the norm for worship (the *lex orandi*), acceptability to the community of believers (the *sensus fidelium*), agreement with the past teaching of popes and councils, and the approval of the contemporary magisterium'.

12. Cf. Dulles, ibid., p. 191: 'Protestant Scripture scholars recognized that Holy Scripture depends heavily on a prior oral tradition, of which it is a privileged sedimentation. Protestants also recognized that they themselves read

Scripture in the light of tradition, and that it is practically impossible to bypass tradition and approach Scripture, as it were, for the first time'. And Paul Tillich is quoted: 'the radical biblicistic attitude is a self-deception'.

13. Ibid., p. 192.

14. *DV* 11. Cf. A. Grillmeier, 'The Divine Inspiration and the Interpretation of Sacred Scripture', in *Commentary* (see note 5), pp. 199–246, esp. 204–215, where an elaborate report is given of the discussions on the *veritas salutaris* and the *veritates profanae* in the Bible. 'Only in order to avoid any misuse of the expression "truth of salvation" (in the sense of a limitation of inspiration, as we can see from the context), is the change made from *veritas salutaris* to "the truth that is written in sacred books for the sake of our salvation"' (p. 234).

15. Cf. *DV* 10: '*Ecclesiae Magisterium ... cuius auctoritas in nomine Jesu exercetur. Quod quidem Magisterium non supra verbum Dei est, sed eidem ministrat, docens nonnisi quod traditum est ...*'

16. Grillmeier, 'Divine Inspiration' (n. 14), p. 226.

17. Cf. the Address of Pope John Paul (see note 4), no. 16: 'I have the joy of being able to offer to Catholic exegetes ... both my thanks and encouragement'.

18. Cf. Ratzinger, 'Dogmatic Constitution' (n. 5), p. 169: '... we might perhaps see the relation of this text to its predecessors as a perfect example of dogmatic development, of the inner *relecture* of dogma in dogmatic history'. Is this not a forced reconciliatory view?

19. Even Catholics may wonder at the casualness with which both inspiration and assistance of the Spirit are claimed.

20. Cf. Ratzinger, 'Dogmatic Constitution' (n. 5), p. 264: 'The barriers ... had been erected from the 13th, and especially from the 15th, century against the Bible in the vernacular and the reading of it by those who were not theologians...' and '... the fight against the Reformation had led to a sequestration of Scripture'. See also, e.g. Lyonnet, 'Chapitres IV et VI' (n. 7), pp. 2000–2001: with regard to the

'restrictions imposées': *'nous sommes gênés, voire scandalisés'*.

21. Ratzinger points out two instances of an 'over-optimistic' attitude. (1) The salvation historical overview in *DV* 3 does not refer to God's wrath and judgement although reference is made to Romans 1-2 (see 'Dogmatic Constitution', pp. 173–174); (2) In discussing *DV* 9 he writes: '... we shall have to acknowledge the truth of the criticism that there is, in fact, no explicit mention of the possibility of a distorting tradition and of the place of Scripture as an element within the Church that is *also* critical of tradition ... That this opportunity has been missed can only be regarded as an unfortunate omission' (Ibid., pp. 192–193).

22. Cf. Bieringer, 'Biblical Revelation' (n. 5), p. 25: 'Can *Dei verbum* offer a new impetus today so that the Bible in the Church can be more what it is and actually should be?'

23. Cf. the comprehensive study of *The Interpretation of the Bible in the Church* by Williamson, *Catholic Principles* (n. 5).

24. Cf. Williamson, *Catholic Principles* (n. 5), pp. 219–252: 'The Use of the Historical-Critical Method'. For this first problem as well as the second see J.A. Fitzmyer, 'Problems of the Literal and Spiritual Senses of Scripture', *Louvain Studies* 20 (1995), pp. 134–146; and 'Concerning the Interpretation of the Bible in the Church', *Josephinum. Journal of Theology* 6 (1999), pp. 5–20.

25. See the thorough analysis of *Dei verbum* 12 in Bieringer, 'Biblical Revelation' (n. 5), pp. 27–50.

26. Cf. *DV* 10: 'But the task of giving an authentic interpretation of the Word of God, whether in its written form or in the form of Tradition, has been entrusted to the living teaching office of the Church alone. Its authority in this matter is exercised in the name of Jesus Christ. Yet this Magisterium is not superior to the Word of God, but is its servant. It teaches only what has been handed on to it'.

27. Cf. R.J. Neuhaus (ed.), *Biblical Interpretation in Crisis. The Ratzinger Conference on Bible and Church*, Grand Rapids,

1989. The conference of Ratzinger is on pp. 1–23; Brown's paper is on pp. 24–37, his *Addenda* on pp. 37–49.

28. Fitzmyer, 'Concerning the Interpretation' (n. 24), pp. 7–8, writes: 'It is somewhat ironic that, at a time when one was hearing criticism of the historical-critical method of biblical interpretation and repeated calls for other methods to replace it, the Biblical Commission devoted a considerable portion of its document to that mode of interpretation, precisely to put it in a proper perspective'.

29. Cf. the Address of Pope John Paul II, n. 13, p. 18: 'The Catholic exegesis does not have its own exclusive method of interpretation, but starting with the historico-critical basis freed from its philosophical presuppositions or those contrary to the truth of our faith, it makes the most of all the current methods by seeking in each of them the "seeds of the Word"'.

30. Williamson, *Catholic Principles* (n. 4), p. 238.

31. One thinks here of 'the fantasy of the "unpapal conclave"' of J.P. Meier 'to illustrate what a *historical*, as distinct from a *theological*, investigation of Jesus must involve'. See *A Marginal Jew: Rethinking the Historical Jesus. Vol. II: Mentor, Message, and Miracles*, New York 1994, pp. 4–5: 'a Catholic, a Protestant, a Jew, and an agnostic – all honest historians cognizant of 1st century religious movements – are locked up in the bowels of the Harvard Divinity School library, put on a spartan diet, and not allowed to emerge until they have hammered out a consensus document on Jesus of Nazareth'. Cf. also the presendential address by W.A. Meeks at the SNTS Meeting in Barcelona (2004) 'Why Study the New Testament', *NTS* 51 (2005) 155–170. He mentions 'the arrogance of fideist hermeneutics, which insists that in order truly to understand our texts you must first convert' (p. 169).

32. Yet one must take into account that an exegete cannot do all things. One should thus distinguish between a (complete) exegesis and the (specialised) exegete. The criticism of onesidedness, however, applies to today's exegesis as a whole.

33. Cf. Williamson, *Catholic Principles* (n. 4), pp. 248–251. Williamson finishes the chapter on 'The Use of the Historical-Critical Method' as follows: 'Despite the Biblical Commission's achievement in articulating an approach to the historical-critical method that is compatible with Catholic principles of interpretation, this section has identified two weaknesses in the Biblical Commission's treatment of this topic. First, the *IBC* glosses over problematic presuppositions that still often accompany the use of the historical-critical method and that are considered by some scholars to be intrinsic to it. Unfortunately, by failing to distinguish sharply enough between the approach to the historical-critical method they endorse and other approaches that enjoy wide currency, the Biblical Commission's position has been widely misunderstood as an almost unqualified endorsement of the historical-critical method.

    'The second weakness of the *IBC*'s treatment of the historical-critical method was its failure to treat a variety of questions regarding the relation of history to the interpretation of the Bible in the Church. Although this is not a new topic and has been treated at various times in the past, it remains one of the most important problems raised by the historical-critical method, and it has practical ramifications for theology, exegesis, and pastoral care.' (pp. 251–252)

34. Cf. the reflective and beautifully written monograph by D.M. Williams, *Receiving the Bible in Faith: Historical and Theological Exegesis*, Washington, D.C., 2004. See also Williamson, *Catholic Principles* (n. 4), pp. 161–215: 'The Meaning of Inspired Scripture'; the two articles of Fitzmyer mentioned in n. 21; and Bieringer, 'Biblical Revelation' (n. 5), pp. 27–52 on *DV* 12 (on pp. 44–50 he briefly discusses the opinions of A. Grillmeier, J. Gnilka, N. Lohfink, G. O'Collins, I. de la Potterie and J. Ratzinger).

35. Cf., e.g. Williams, *Receiving the Bible in Faith* (n. 34), pp. 62–63; Fitzmyer, 'Problems' (n. 24), p. 125. See also M.A. Powell, 'Authorial Intent and Historical Reporting: Putting Spong's Literalization Thesis to the Test', *Journal for the Study of the Historical Jesus* 2 (2003), pp. 225–249.

36. We may quote here also Ratzinger's reflection on modern hermeneutics in 'Dogmatic Constitution' (n. 5), pp. 187–188: 'a deeper knowledge of the problem of human understanding, which is no longer adequately expressed by the simple ideas of a given fact and its explanation, because the explanation as the process of understanding cannot be clearly separated from what is being understood. This interdependence of the two, which does not remove the ultimate basic difference between assimilation and what is assimilated, even if they can no longer be strictly isolated, is well expressed by the dialectic juxtapositiion of the two clauses *Traditio proficit* and *crescit perceptio (DV* 8)'. *DV* 8 states: 'The Tradition that comes from the apostles *makes progress* in the Church, with the help of the Holy Spirit. There *is growth in insight* into the realities and words that are being passed on'.

   The term 'supernatural' appears to be avoided in *Dei verbum*. Cf. Ratzinger, ibid., pp. 179–180. However, in *DV* 6 the verb *superare* is present in a quotation from Vatican I: 'to share with us divine benefits which entirely *surpass* the powers of the human mind to understand'.

   One is reminded of E. Schillebeeckx' well-known double thesis: no revelation without experience; no experience without interpretation. Cf., e.g. P. De Mey, 'The Relation between Revelation and Experience in *Dei verbum*. An Evaluation in the Light of Postconciliar Theology', in *Vatican II and Its Legacy* (n. 5), pp. 95–105, esp. 99–101.

37. Can a text possess a completely 'autonomous' meaning?

38. Meeks, 'Why Study the New Testament' (n. 31), p. 166, complains: 'deconstructionists have thrown the text to the mercy of the reader'.

39. I doubt that in this context '*Polyvalenz*' (plurality of meanings) is the correct term. See the recent study by H. Roose, 'Polyvalenz durch Intertextualität im Spiegel der aktuellen Forschung zu den Tessalonicherbriefen', *NTS* 51 (2005), pp. 250–269.

40. Since *DV* addresses believers, we do not deal in this paper with the problem of those who cannot accept divine authorship. See, however, note 44.
41. Williamson, *Catholic Principles* (n. 4), p. 180. Cf. Bieringer, 'Biblical Revelation' (n. 5), esp. pp. 33 and 3839.
42. Cf. Williams, *Receiving the Bible in Faith* (n. 34), p. 196: 'The formal principle of the canon and the material principle of the centrality of Christ function as the main indicators of the divine intention within Scripture'.
43. The spiritual sense must, of course, be distinguished from the 'accommodated' sense. Cf. Fitzmyer, 'Problems' (n. 24), pp. 139–140.
44. Hence in his two studies Fitzmyer speaks of the spiritual sense as classical, traditional and Christological.
45. Cf. I. Finkelstein and N.A. Silberman, *The Bible Unearthed: Archaeology's New Vision of Ancient Israel and the Origin of Its Sacred Texts*, New York, 2001.
46. The distinction between believer and unbeliever may be too simplistic, since in all believers faith and doubt (and unbelief) struggle.
47. Cf. U. Vanni, 'Exégèse et actualisation à la lumière de *Dei verbum*', in *Vatican II* (n. 7), pp. 351–369.
48. Fitzmyer, 'Concerning the Interpretation' (n. 24), p. 17.
49. The opinion of Fitzmyer, ibid., p. 19, probably is too strict: 'Any actualized meaning that does not have such a homogeneous connection with what was meant or with the literal sense becomes, in effect, an extraneous sense foisted on the Word of God. It thus becomes eisegesis, the opposite of exegesis'.
50. Cf. Dulles, 'Revelation, Theology of' (n. 10), p. 196: 'Some theologians hold that the Bible, like the preached word, has quasi-sacramental value; that is, that one who reads or hears it under favorable circumstances receives grace to enter into a new relationship with God in faith'.
51. See R. Bieringer, 'The Spirit's Guidance into All the Truth. The Text-critical Problems of John 16,13', in A. Denaux (ed.), *New Testament Textual Criticism and Exegesis. FS J.*

Delobel (BETL 161), Leuven 2002, pp. 183–207, on the variant readings and his choice for *eis tèn alètheian* (not *en thè alètheia*) and *akousei* (not *akouei*).

52. Ratzinger, *Commentary* (see n. 5), p. 268 (with reference to H. Schelkle).

A Renewed Theology of Divine Revelation: Response to Jan Lambrecht

Thomas Norris

I. A New Perspective

In his paper, Professor Lambrecht very appropriately reminded us of certain facts that are vital to understanding the Constitution on Divine Revelation, *Dei verbum*. He highlighted a sequence of redactions before its final acceptance by the Council. In fact, its gestation was coterminous with the four sessions of Vatican Two. The first schema, *De fontibus revelationis*, set out from the debate concerning Scripture and Tradition in their rapport with divine revelation. That schema also read the two categories in the light not so much of Trent as *of the Counter-Reformation*. Professor Lambrecht showed that in delicately side-stepping that debate the Council was able to adopt a fresh perspective. The new perspective consisted in a better understanding of the reality of divine revelation. The first chapter of *Dei verbum* addresses this substantial issue.

However, it is perhaps worth considering in greater detail the implications of the new status given to revelation in the unfolding elaboration of the Constitution. There was an enormous shift from understanding revelation as the disclosure of doctrines to understanding revelation as the communication of the divine life: 'In his goodness and wisdom, God chose to reveal himself and to make known the hidden purpose of his will by which through Christ, the Word made flesh, we have access to the Father in the Holy Spirit and come to share in the divine nature' (*DV* 2).

The idea of revelation here is that of divine self-communication: the life of God is that of the Holy Trinity, and it is precisely that Trinitarian life that is offered to us. This is the holistic view of revelation that Professor Lambrecht rightly considers remarkable. Revelation is the free act of the Trinity by which the Divine Three opened up their life to us in order to draw us out of death and despair, and into their very communion.

This notion of divine self-communication is stressed in the *overture* of *Dei verbum* where the First Letter of John is quoted: 'We announce to you the eternal life which was with the Father, and has appeared to us. What we have seen and heard we announce to you, in order that you may have fellowship [*koinonia*] with us, and that our fellowship may be with the Father, and with his Son Jesus Christ' (*DV* 2–3). The divine *koinonia* of the Three breaks upon the world 'so that men and women have access to the Father in the Holy Spirit and come to share in the divine nature' (*DV* 2).

The deceased theologian and bishop, Klaus Hemmerle, wrote that the Trinity makes the Church into its created heaven, while the Trinity remains the uncreated heaven of the Church.'[1] It seems to me that the theology of revelation of *Dei verbum* is nothing less than this *admirabile commercium* as between the mystery of the Trinity and the mystery of the Church.

In beginning with a renewed theology of divine revelation, the Council freed itself from a context of controversy. It set forth the mystery of faith (Rom 16:25;

Eph 3:4-6; Col 1:26-7) without involving itself at once and irretrievably in the Scripture–Tradition debate as the primary issue. Such a clear and dynamic idea of divine revelation opens up for the Council new vistas that had been unknown for centuries: '... this plan of revelation is realised by deeds and words having an inner unity' (*gestis verbisque intrinsice inter se connexis*). Revelation, therefore, is realised in events, gestures and words that are recapitulated in the Event of Jesus Christ, who is 'both the mediator and the fullness of all revelation' (*DV* 2). Furthermore, section 4 identifies the events of the paschal mystery as the perfection and summit of revelation: where the Word-made-flesh is un-worded,[2] as it were, there *the Deed* of death and resurrection speaks most powerfully, becoming in truth the all-encompassing 'word of the Cross' (1 Cor 1:18). This fact opens up the possibility of harmonising Scripture and Tradition, for is not the former the written Word while the latter is dispensed by 'the Church [who] in her teaching, life, and worship perpetuates and hands on to all generations all that she herself is, all that she believes' (*DV* 8)?

II. A Fuller Sense of the Word of God

Such an understanding of revelation points the Church towards the unfathomable riches contained in divine revelation as the Word of the living God living among men and women and so making history. The term, 'Word of God', is used throughout as a synonym for divine revelation. Little wonder, then, that the very opening words of the text are, '*Dei verbum*'. In the official Latin text, these words are in the upper case. Commentators stress that fact, for it shows that the Council did not want to deal with the *written* Word of God exclusively; *Dei verbum* is not a treatise about sacred scripture only, nor about tradition only, nor primarily about their relationship. Rather, it is an ecumenical council's methodological study of the fundamental and grounding categories of Christianity beginning with revelation as the Word of God, and the event of Jesus Christ who gives a personal name to that revelation.

Vatican II did that by means of a 'Christological concentration', which showed the Council the way to open up, at one stroke, a perspective and an approach to the battle engrossing Catholics and Protestants since the Reformation. Henri de Lubac wrote the preface for Roger Schutz's and Max Thurian's commentary on *Dei verbum* in 1996. He says: 'The Word of God is the living Christ whom God gives to humanity, in order to establish between himself and them, and between themselves, the communion of the Spirit in the Church.'[3] Consequently, 'revelation is the initial and essential idea of Christianity.'[4]

III. Scripture and Tradition: The Media of Divine Revelation as Dispensed by the Church

The transmission of divine revelation is a matter of salvation for all nations. Revelation in fact communicates a reality that heals, a grace that uplifts and a way of life that is to be followed by those who believe. The Council describes how 'God, in his gracious goodness, has seen to it that what he had revealed for the salvation of all nations would abide perpetually in its full integrity and be handed on to all generations' (*DV 7*). The perpetual abiding and handing on of divine revelation necessarily highlight the task of finding a better understanding of scripture, tradition and magisterium. A renewed theology of revelation is in place, indeed, but that requires a renewed theology of scripture, tradition and magisterium, especially since the Council wished to revisit formally those foundational first categories of the faith.

It is little wonder, then, that in section 9, these categories are described via the Word of God, via Revelation. They must in fact be defined in terms of revelation, indeed, as the media or carriers of divine revelation and the Word of God. They are its servants. Thus 'sacred Scripture *is* the Word of God (*locutio Dei*) inasmuch as it is consigned to writing under the influence of the divine Spirit'. For its part, sacred tradition 'hands on to the successors of the Apostles in its full purity God's word [*Verbum Dei*] which was entrusted to the apostles by Christ the Lord and the Holy Spirit' (*DV* 9). Tradition, then, consists in Christ's fidelity to the Church, as the historical blossoming of the People of Israel (Gal 6:16) and the Church's Spirit-inspired desire to remember and to respond.

I found Professor Lambrecht's exposition of the 1993 Pontifical Biblical Commission's document on the employment of the historical-critical method in scriptural interpretation both vigorous and nuanced. In that setting the biblical categories of *anamnesis* and *diakonia* came to mind: the *anamnesis* of actualisation and the *diakonia* of 'the obedience of faith'. Such a combination would make Christians not only critical 'hearers of the written Word' but also 'doers of the same Word' (James 1:21-5).

To sum up, *Dei verbum* provides an inspiring theology of divine revelation to the extent that the Constitution is primary evidence for the claim that Vatican II was not only a pastoral council, but also a richly theological one; that theology throws a clarifying light over the constitutive categories of scripture, tradition and magisterium. We now have a fresh understanding of these fundamental categories of faith. And that should be an exceptional benefit for biblical exegesis in the years and decades that lie ahead.

Notes

1. K. Hemmerle, 'Trinitarische Kirche – Kirche als Communio' in *Gemeinsam fuer die Menscheit*. Internationaler Priesterkongress 1988, Neue-Stadt-Dokumentation 2, Muenchen 1988, pp. 43–61.
2. See Hans Urs von Balthasar, *Herrlickheit, III, 2/II*, Einsiedeln 1969, section 'Nichtwort als Mitte des Wortes,' pp. 69–81.
3. *La parole vivante au Concile*, Taize 1996, p. 220.
4. John Henry Newman, *Via Media*, Vol. I, London, New York, Bombay 1901, p. xlvii.

The Relationship between the Old Testament and the New Testament According to *Dei verbum*[1]

Beate Kowalski

Exegetes read *Dei verbum* forty years after its promulgation in a different way than that of the time of Vatican II.[2] Having studied exegesis after Vatican II and being trained in various exegetical methodologies, I believe *Dei verbum* is already an historical document outdated by more recent documents of the Pontifical Biblical Commission. As I am very much interested in intertextuality I read *Dei verbum* from the perspective of the relationship between the Old Testament and New Testament (hereafter, OT and NT).[3] Of course, that was not the intention of the constitution, but it is worthwhile to study the document under this aspect in order to portray recent developments in exegesis.[4] A few critical insights will be presented in what follows.

Dei verbum[5]
The general chapter (III: 'Sacred Scripture, its inspiration and divine interpretation') deals with the divine nature of Scripture and the relationship between inspiration and human authorship first. It claims that both parts of Scripture, all books of the OT and NT in their entirety, are considered to be sacred and canonical (*libros enim integros*

tam Veteris quam Novi Testamenti, cum omnibus eorum partibus ... pro sacris et canonicis habet) (III, 11).[6] This statement includes the OT and appreciates its value. The following chapter 4 then focuses on the OT itself. A more distinguished view on the OT becomes discernible.

Chapter 4 (*De vetere Testamento*), Article 14
After a short description of God's history of salvation in the OT (chosen people, covenant, prophets), the document states that:

> The plan of salvation foretold (*praenuntiata*) by the sacred authors, recounted and explained by them, is found as the true word of God in the books of the Old Testament: these books, therefore, written under divine inspiration, remain permanently valuable (*perennem valorem servant*). (Article 14)

Again, the divine nature of the OT is mentioned. Futhermore, the permanent value of the first part of the Bible is emphasised. It is quite strange and contrary to these statements that only a very small amount of OT references are used in *Dei verbum*, most of them are to be found in article 14. There is only one direct quotation from the OT in the whole document. Furthermore, article 14 closes with a quotation from Rom 15:4.

Though dealing with the OT, chapter 4 argues with NT references that refer back to the OT. The perspective of this chapter is reading the OT in the light of its reception in the NT. Above all, the references referred to in article 14 offer a very small selection of the rich OT tradition. Two refer to God's covenant with Abraham and Moses (Gen 15:18), the universal perspective of God's covenant with the peoples as part of the book of Psalms and prophetic writings is mentioned but not in terms of a covenant (Ps 21:29; 95:1-3; Is 2:1-5; Jer 3:17).[7] Nothing is said about the wisdom tradition and other theological aspects of the OT.

Figure 7.1: OT/NT Allusions and Quotations in
Dei verbum[8]

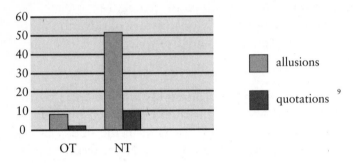

allusions

quotations [9]

Chapter 4, Article 15
The purpose of the OT is described in a threefold manner in article 15:

> The principal purpose to which the plan of the old covenant was directed was to prepare for the coming of Christ, the redeemer of all and of the messianic kingdom, to announce this coming by prophecy (see Lk 24:44; Jn 5:39; 1 Peter 1:10), and to indicate its meaning through various types (see 1 Cor 10:12).

Thus, the OT is to prepare (*praepararet*) for the coming of Christ, to announce this coming by prophecy (*prophetice nuntiaret*) and to indicate its meaning through various types (*et variis typis significaret*). Again, the OT is just read in the light of Christ. It does not have its own value other than announcing, preparing and prophesying the Messiah. All the rich faith experiences of Israel during its journey through history are omitted. Implicitly a selection of the more important texts of the OT is made by this. Only those text segments dealing with the covenant and the annunciation of the Messiah seem to be important. It is not certain if this was the intention of the Council Fathers, but one can come to this conclusion.

Figure 7.2: Purpose of the OT According to
Dei verbum **IV, 15**

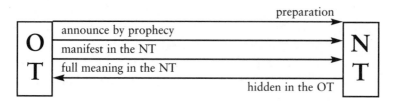

A very negative view on the OT is taken in the final paragraph of article 15.

> These books, though they also contain some things which are incomplete and temporary (*imperfecta et temporaria contineant*), nevertheless show us true divine pedagogy (*paedagogiam divinam demonstrant*).

This means that the OT needs the NT in terms of completion and indefinite value. It seems to be of lower quality than the writings of the NT. The criterion for this view is not explicitly mentioned, but it is quite obvious from the context: the Christ event. Nevertheless, *Dei verbum* states that the OT contains wisdom, prayers and the mystery of our salvation in a hidden way (*in quibus tandem latet mysterium salutis nostrae*).

Chapter 4, Article 16

The final article describes the relationship between both testaments more precisely:

> God, the inspirer and author of both Testaments, wisely arranged that the New Testament be hidden in the Old (*ut Novum in Vetere lateret*) and the Old be made manifest in the New (*in Novo Vetus pateret*).

> ... still the books of the Old Testament with all their parts, caught up into the proclamation of the Gospel, (3) acquire and show forth their full meaning in the New Testament [*significationem suam completam acquirunt et ostendunt*] (see Mt 5:17; Lk 24:27; Rom 16:25-26; 2 Cor 14:16) and in turn shed light on it and explain it.

Again it is obvious that the OT is understood and read in the light of the NT. There is only one full meaning of the OT in so far as it is caught up with the proclamation of the Gospel. The reading direction is from the OT to the NT, but the OT does not seem to have its own value.

Let me conclude: *Dei verbum* has a general positive view on the OT. Its writings are regarded as written under divine inspiration and remain permanently valuable. Christians should receive them with reverence. Compared with former times, when the OT was on the index of forbidden books, this is a huge step forward.

But *Dei verbum* is a document of its time and it has limits. Although the Council Fathers spoke highly of the OT, they stayed with the old model of promise and fulfilment. It is a compromise that appreciates the OT writings on the one hand, and reads them just in the light of the Christ event on the other hand. Although Vatican II made a huge step forward towards a better understanding between Jews and Christians (see *Nostrae Aetate*) it remains with the old view on the OT which is handed down since Marcion's time. Futhermore, the constitution uses Scripture as a proof-text which is another critical aspect.

The Pontifical Biblical Commission, *The Jewish People and their Sacred Scriptures in the Christian Bible* (2001)
In 2001 the Pontifical Biblical Commission published a document entitled *The Jewish People and their Sacred Scriptures in the Christian Bible*. It deals with the unity of both parts of the Bible, describes different aspects of their relationship towards each other and discusses some problematic aspects. The troubled relationship between Jews and Christians and in particular the persecution of Jews during the Second World War motivated the members of the Commission to reflect on the relationship between both parts of Scripture in a new way. They took into account modern results of exegesis of the past twenty years, especially the results of canonical approaches and Jewish exegesis.[10] Furthermore, research into the presentation of Jews and anti-judaistic aspects were consulted. The document not only presents theoretical reflections, but concludes with some general and pastoral orientations to improve the relationship between Jews and Christians.

Compared with *Dei verbum* the document is revolutionary as it contains a variety of perspectives on the OT. A few aspects of the document are mentioned here. The relationship between the two parts of Scripture is now described as a reciprocal and inseparable one. The NT demands to be read in the light of the OT, but it also invites a re-reading of the OT in the light of Jesus Christ.[11] Thus, there are two ways of reading the OT, and both have their own value: there is an original meaning and understanding of the OT at the time of its writing and at the same time it can be read as a subsequent interpretation in the light of Christ.[12]

The document states that there is a unity between the two parts of Scripture. There is continuity and discontinuity between the various traditions.[13] The old model of promise and fulfilment cannot be used any more to describe the relationship between the two parts of Scripture. Some promises are already fulfilled in the OT[14], others are mentioned for the first time in the NT[15]. Furthermore, the image of God cannot be described as a God of violence in the OT and a God of love in the NT.[16]

To summarise, the recent document develops further the positive ideas of *Dei verbum*. It intends to improve the relationship between Jews and Christians. The rich traditions of the OT and the different ways to read them – from a Jewish and a Christian perspective – are appreciated. Nevertheless, the document has weaknesses. It sometimes presents too positive an interpretation of anti-judaistic tendencies in the NT.[17] But that is another matter and a topic for further reflection. In terms of the relationship between OT and NT the document has set, or officially confirmed, a new step in exegesis.

Notes

1. Response to Jan Lambrecht's paper delivered on 25 October 2005 at Mater Dei Institute, Dublin, and on 27 October 2005 at Mary Immaculate College, Limerick. This paper is also printed in an Irish Biblical Association's publication, edited by Kieran O'Mahony,
2. Among the many publications on *Dei verbum* only a very few can be mentioned here: An international congress ('Sacred Scripture in the Life of the Church') took place in Rome from 14–18 September 2005, organised by the Catholic Biblical Federation and the Pontifical Council for

Promoting Christian Unity to celebrate the fortieth anniversary of the promulgation of the Vatican II Dogmatic Constitution on Divine Revelation *Dei verbum*. The lectures delivered at this congress are published on the website of the CBF (*www.deiverbum2005.org*). A few recent publications can be listed here: R. Bieringer, *Biblical Revelation and Exegetical Interpretation According to Dei verbum 12*, in: SNTU 27 (2002) 5–40; D. Kosch, *Um unseres Heiles willen. Eine relecture von "Dei verbum" nach 40 Jahren*, in: BiKi 60/1 (2005) 45–50; H. Frankemölle, *Fortschritte und Stillstand. Entwicklungen seit 1965*, in: BiKi 60/3 (2005) 173–177, who also presents his thoughts on the two recent documents of the Pontifical Biblical Commission.

3. As far as I know, only one publication deals with this topic, cf. G. Castello, *Antico Testamento e rapporto con gli Ebrei. Una rilettura del capitolo IV della Dei verbum*, in: Asprenas 50, 2–4 (2003), pp. 79–104.

4. Just to mention three aspects of this development. Firstly, Jewish studies (e.g. Yair Zakovitch, *Das Buch Ruth. Ein jüdischer Kommentar* (SBS 177), Stuttgart 1999) and a new view on the OT (cf. e.g. E. Zenger, *Das Erste Testament. Die jüdische Bibel und die Christen*, Düsseldorf 1992; E. Zenger, *Am Fuß des Sinai. Gottesbilder des Ersten Testaments*, Düsseldorf 1993). Secondly, the so-named canonical approach – well known and connected with B.S. Childs (*Old Testament Theology in a Canonical Context*, London 1985, *Biblical Theology of the Old and New Testaments: Theological Reflection on the Christian Bible*, London 1996); cf. further D.L. Baker, *Two Testaments, one Bible. Study of the theological relationship between the Old and New Testaments*, Leicester 21991. And thirdly, studies in intertextuality which are especially developed among English and Scandinavian scholars (cf. e.g. S. Moyise (ed.), *The Old Testament in the New Testament. Essays in Honour of J.L. North* (JSNT.S 189) Sheffield 2000) and publications by M.J. Menken, two international leading scholars on intertextuality.

5. Cf. the English translation of *Dei verbum*: H. Vorgrimler (ed.), *Commentary on the Documents of Vatican II*. Vol. III, New York/London, 1969, pp. 155–272: 'Dogmatic Constitution on Divine Revelation'. The Latin quotation are taken from H. Denzinger, *Enchiridion symbolorum defititionum et declarationum de rebus fidei et morum. Kompendium der Glaubensbekenntnisse und kirchlichen Lehrentscheidungen. Lateinisch – Deutsch*, P. Hünermann, Freiburg/Basel/Rom/Wien (eds)1991.

6. 'For holy mother Church, relying on the belief of the Apostles (see John 20:31; 2 Tim 3:16; 2 Peter 1:19-20, 3:15-16), holds that the books of both the Old and New Testaments in their entirety, with all their parts, are sacred and canonical because written under the inspiration of the Holy Spirit, they have God as their author and have been handed on as such to the Church herself.' (*DV* 11)

7. Cf. N. Lohfink/E. Zenger, *Der Gott Israels und die Völker. Untersuchungen zum Jesajabuch und zu den Psalmen* (SBS 154), Stuttgart 1994.

8. A precise analysis of the NT allusions and quotations reveals a strong use of John's Gospel (12 allusions, 1 direct quotation). The direct quotations are taken from Jn (1), Acts (1), Rom (3), Phil (1), 2 Thess (1), 2 Tim (1), Hebr (2). The OT allusions are taken from Gen (2), Ex (2), Ps (2), Isa (1), Jer (1), Bar (1). The comparison between the use of OT and NT comes to the result of 9 allusions to the OT and 52 to the NT, 1 quotation from OT and 10 from NT.

9. The statistics of allusions and quotations from Scripture is quite interesting in so far as out of 61 allusions in total 52 are from the NT (John's Gospel is on the top), out of 11 quotations only 1 is from the OT. A clear preference for one OT writing is not discernible. Gen, Ex and Ps are each used twice, Isa, Jer and Bar are used once.

10. Cf. the chapter on 'Jewish exegetical methods employed in the New Testament' (including sub-chapters on Jewish methods of exegesis, exegesis at Qumran and in the NT, rabbinic methods in the NT, important allusions to the OT).

11. J. Paulien speaks about a 'further-reading' of the OT (within his review of my Habilitationsschrift [B. Kowalski, Die Rezeption des Propheten Ezechiels in der Offenbarung des Johannes (SBB 52), Stuttgart 2004], which will be published in JBL).

12. Cf. the second part of the document 'Fundamental themes in the Jewish Scriptures and their reception into faith in Christ', especially the first part 'Christian understanding of the relationship between the OT and NT' (affirmation of reciprocal relationship, re-reading the OT in the light of Christ, allegorical re-reading, return to the literal sense, unity of God's plan and the idea of fulfilment, current perspectives, contribution to Jewish reading of the Bible).

13. Cf. the conclusions dealing with continuity, discontinuity, and progression.

14. E.g. the promises to Abraham in Gen 12:2, 3.

15. E.g. Jesus' promise of the eternal life and the resurrection of the dead.

16. The image of a loving God is already to be found in the OT (e.g. Hos 2:21, 22; 11:3, 4), whereas the NT also announces the last judgment (e.g. Mt 25:31-46).

17. Cf. the conclusion of the chapter on the Jews in the Gospels and Acts of the Apostles: 'The Gospels reveal that the fulfilment of God's plan necessarily brought with it a confrontation with evil, which must be eradicated from the human heart. This confrontation puts Jesus at odds with the leaders of his people, just like the ancient prophets. Already in the Old Testament, the people of God were seen under two antithetical aspects: on the one hand, as a people called to be perfectly united to God; and on the other, as a sinful people. These two aspects could not fail to manifest themselves during Jesus' ministry. During the Passion, the negative aspect seemed to prevail, even among the Twelve. But the resurrection showed that, in reality, the love of God was victorious and obtained for all the pardon of sin and a new life.' With regard to the painful Wirkungsgeschichte of some anti-judaistic tendencies in the NT writings (e.g. Mt 27:25; Jn 8:44) and recent publications this seems to be a too positive view on a very serious matter.

Religious Education since Vatican II: Significant Voices

Maura Hyland

To set the scene I will begin by looking briefly at how religious education was taught before Vatican II. Religious education has never existed in a vacuum. The way in which it has been taught reflects the educational and theological mindset of a particular time. It has been influenced by particular world views and certain ways of life. I would like to read a passage from John McGahern's *Memoir*:

> Religion and religious imagery were part of the air we breathed. Prayers were said each morning. Work and talk stopped in fields and houses and school and shop and the busy street at the first sound of the Angelus bell each day at noon. Every day was closed with the Rosary at night. The worlds to come, hell and heaven and purgatory and limbo, were closer and far more real than America or Australia and talked about almost daily as our future reality.
>
> Heaven was in the sky. My mother spoke to me of heaven as concretely and with as much love as she named the wild flowers. Above us the sun of heaven shone. Beyond the sun was the gate of heaven. Within

the gates were the thrones and mansions, the Three Persons in the One God, the Blessed Virgin, the angels and saints, and beyond those mansions were the gardens of paradise where time ceased and everything entered an instant of joy that lasted for all eternity at one with the mind of God. It was her prayer and fervent hope that we would all live there together in happiness with God for all eternity.

Heaven was in the sky. Hell was in the bowels of the earth. There, eternal fire raged. The souls of the damned had to dwell in hell through all eternity, deprived for ever of the sight of the face of God. At its entrance was a great river. Across a wide plain, naked and weeping, came the souls of the damned from the Judgement Seat, bearing only a single coin to give to the boatman to take them across the river into eternal fire.

Between this hell and heaven, purgatory was placed. Descriptions of it were vague, probably because all of us expected to spend time there. The saints alone went straight to heaven. In purgatory, we would have to be purified in flame to a whiteness like that of snow before we could join the saints in the blessedness of heaven.

Away in a silent corner was limbo, where grave-faced children who hadn't received baptism slept, without consciousness or pain, throughout all eternity. Limbo was closed to us because of our baptism. In those young years, contemplating a future hell, or at best the long purifications of purgatory, it did not seem a bad place at all, and there were times when I hoped that some essential rite had been overlooked during my baptism; but I could not communicate this to my mother.

In that context there was a coherence between life as it was lived and peoples' religious faith. There was a certain inbuilt security. Change, if it happened, came slowly. Knowledge was there to be acquired. It existed in a body which with time was accessible.

At that time the major catechetical methodology was based on the use of the catechism. The catechism contained a summary of Christian beliefs and principles, often presented in easily memorised question-and-answer form. This methodology evolved from a concern on the part of the Church, in the period after the reformation, to preserve doctrinal and moral truth and to eliminate error. It was claimed by Edward Rogan that in Ireland from the mid-nineteenth to the mid-twentieth centuries use of the catechism led to a situation which he described as follows: 'Irish Catholics in general were instructed in the truths of their religion with a thoroughness previously unseen in Ireland.'[1]

In the period immediately after the Reformation, catechisms were written in the main for the use of the clergy, with the intention of helping them to make links between the gospel message and official Church teaching or doctrine. When catechisms began to be designed for the classroom they presented the doctrine in a simpler more condensed form and in an easily memorised question-and-answer format. The catechism is still regarded as an important catechetical tool, where those interested can gain easy access to the Church's teaching on any particular question. To this end in 1994, the *Catechism of the Catholic Church* was published as 'a reference text' for 'the entire Church'.

In the school context, the advantages of the catechism were seen to be: it presented Church teaching with a clarity which ruled out any confusion as to what teachers should teach or what children should learn, and it was easy to ascertain whether or not a particular body of material had in fact been learned. However, one would have to wonder whether the desired clarity was for the benefit of those whose responsibility it was to determine what and how much should be learned by a child at a particular age or for the benefit of the child for whom clarity must have been impossible in relation to the meaning of some of the concepts presented and the language used in the catechism. It presented to children answers they did not understand to questions they did not have.

In Irish schools from the early 1950s it was *The Maynooth Catechism*, published in 1951, or catechisms based on *The Maynooth Catechism*, which were used.

An example:

- What are the purposes for which mass is offered?
  The purposes for which mass is offered are: to adore God, to thank him for his benefits, to make satisfaction for our sins and to obtain his grace and blessing.
- How is the Mass the same sacrifice as that of the cross?
  The Mass is the same sacrifice as that of the cross because the same Christ who offered himself a bleeding victim on the cross offers himself in a non-bloody manner by the hands of his priests in the mass.

Brendan Kennelly explores the methodology of religious education as taught by the teacher, Mulcahy, using the catechism:

> Explain the Immaculate Conception, Maguire,
> And then tell us about the Mystical Blood.
> Maguire failed. Mulcahy covered the boy's head

with his satchel, shoved him stumbling among the desks, lashed his bare legs until they bled.[2]

Even before Vatican II dissatisfaction with the Catechism as a catechetical method was growing. It was seen to be too theological for children, the concepts were too difficult, the language was adult in its orientation and what was learned off by heart had little connection with the lived experience of the children.

In the case of Ireland, the first seeds of change came from Germany originating in the work of Jungmann and Hoffinger. This work gave birth to what became known as the Kerygmatic approach. The emphasis in the Kerygmatic approach was on the proclamation of the Good News. Jungman, mindful of the early Church's emphasis on the proclamation of the Good News of Jesus Christ, and convinced that that proclamation should be central to the catechetical endeavour, wanted to move away from what he saw as an over-indulgence on the part of the Church in a post-reformation defensive stance. The Kerygmatic approach emphasises the proclamation of the Word of God, as it is expressed in the Bible, proclaimed and celebrated in the liturgy, witnessed to in the lives of Christians and formulated in the teaching of the Church. Kerygmatic Catechesis is seen as the joyful, challenging proclamation of the Good News which calls for a response of faith and commitment to God. In Ireland, in the first instance, the Kerygmatic approach led to a new emphasis on the Bible. What was then called bible history was introduced to both primary and secondary schools in the 1950s. In the 1960s some local texts were developed in a number of Irish dioceses, for example Ossory, Limerick, Dublin and Raphoe. There was also for the first time a recognition of the importance of what were termed visual aids in religious education. The *On Our Way* series, which typified a Kerygmatic approach, and which originated in the USA, was introduced into some Irish schools in the 1960s and 1970s. In the 1960s Vatican II marked a watershed in the life of the Church. In Ireland, however, the 1960s was a time of dawning awareness in a number of areas. In 1961 television arrived in Ireland. Programmes, probably most notably *The Late Late Show*, led Irish people to question hitherto unquestioned social, political and religious orthodoxies. Ireland's membership of the European Union was anticipated. In 1960 female workers received 53 per cent of the male rate.[3] In a context where inequality was still accepted in many areas, including the rate of pay, the Commission on the Status of Women was founded in 1969.

A lot of attention has been focused on the rigidity of Archbishop John Charles McQuaid of Dublin. At the same time, however, Bishop Lucy of Cork was vocal about the marginalisation of rural communities, public health issues and on the connection between business and politics. Bishop Birch of Ossory developed a new approach to the administration of social services in Kilkenny. While many Irish people were comfortable according to European standards, there was a recognition that social services had not kept pace with economic development, resulting in deprivation in areas such as education and health. In the education system, in 1964 state capital grants for secondary schools were introduced, as were state-funded comprehensive schools. A common Intermediate Course was introduced in 1966. Some reduction in class numbers in primary schools was also introduced. Patrick Hillery, who was minister for education between 1959 and 1965, introduced a scholarship scheme for third level in 1962. In 1964 only 36 per cent of 16-year-olds and 14 per cent of 18-year-olds were in full-time education. This figure represented 46.5 per cent of children of professional people but only 10 per cent of children of unskilled or semi-skilled workers. In 1966, prompted by figures which showed that the percentage of Irish children between 14 and 19 who were attending full-time education was half the figure for other European countries, Donagh O'Malley introduced free secondary education.

The 1960s was the era of The Beatles and The Rolling Stones, with both groups playing at concerts in Dublin. It was also the time when the first glimpses of a new interest in Irish music and culture became apparent, particularly in the numbers who attended the first Fleadh Ceoil. The 1960s saw a number of Irish writers come to prominence: poet Thomas Kinsella, playwrights Tom Murphy and Eugene McCabe, as well as John McGahern, Brian Moore, Seán Ó Faolain, Brian Friel, Edna O'Brien and others. At the end of the 1960s, the first ventures into the world of space travel were made. For the first time, human beings could see pictures of the planet upon which they lived from outside itself, an event which could only result in a changed world view and a new perspective on the earth.

The world where the catechism fitted, without question as to its suitability as a teaching tool, was changed. Vatican II left a catechetical vacuum. While it did not produce a decree on religious education, it gave rise to new understandings in theology and liturgy which challenged what were present practices and called for new approaches. Post Vatican religious education was deeply influenced by the following council documents: the Dogmatic Constitution on the Church, *Lumen gentium*, the Dogmatic Constitution on the Liturgy, *Sacrosanctum concilium*, the Dogmatic Constitution on Divine Revelation, *Dei verbum*, and the Pastoral Constitution on the Church in the Modern World, *Gaudium et spes*.

In a time when the predominant model of the Church was hierarchical and the practice supported that model, *Lumen gentium* presented rich images of the Church such as Sheepfold, Flock, Cultivated Field, Vine, Building of God, Body of Christ, People of God.[4] It situated the Church in time and history as distinct from outside of time and history, while existing in anticipation of the second coming of Christ. It suggests that the Church has a strong ecumenical nature. *Lumen gentium* acknowledges the hierarchical nature of the Church, but it emphasises the priestly function of service and upholds the priestly role of the laity.

Sacrosanctum concilium encouraged active participation in the liturgy, it identified and encouraged various lay ministries, it fostered use of the vernacular and encouraged adaptation to local culture and circumstances. From the point of view of religious education, most significantly, it recognised the educational role of the liturgy. It states, 'Although Sacred Liturgy is principally the worship of the divine majesty it likewise contains much instruction'.[5] *The Directory for Masses with Children* was published in 1974 to provide guidelines for the celebration of the liturgy with children. The Directory recognised the difficulty faced by those wanting to involve children in the celebration of the mass. 'Liturgical and especially Eucahristic celebrations which of their very nature have an educative value, are scarcely fully effective where children are concerned. The mass may be in their own language, but the words and symbols used are not those they can understand.'[6] It required that 'presidential prayers which have been composed for adults should be so adapted in masses with children that the children will consider them to be expressions of their own religious life'.[7] Perhaps most importantly, it refers to masses for adults at parish level in which a number of children participate: 'In masses of this kind care must be taken not to allow the children to feel neglected because of their inability to participate in or understand what is being done and proclaimed in the celebration. At the very least some account must be taken of their presence.'[8] As a result of this, Eucharistic Prayers for Masses with Children were published. Teachers were encouraged to provide opportunities for children to take part in Eucharistic celebrations which were designed with their participation in mind. However, with some notable exceptions, little happened by way of response to this document at parish level.

Dei verbum explored God's revelation to humankind from biblical and historical perspectives. God's self-revelation comes to us in the first instance through his Son Jesus Christ: 'His will was that we should have access to the Father, through Christ, the Word made flesh, in the Holy Spirit, and thus become sharers in the Divine Nature.'[9] According to *Dei verbum*, scripture and tradition are complementary sources of revelation.

However, we can also 'come to know God with certainty from the natural world, by the natural light of human reason'.[10] Faith is the response to God's revelation, not simply an intellectual response but a response from the heart which influences not only what is known but which also that which shapes peoples' lives.

This understanding of divine revelation had a profound effect on religious education methodologies. It encouraged a focus on sacred scripture, which in turn led to a catechetical methodology which took the word of God as its starting point. It also encouraged religious educators to take seriously the human experience of those being educated since experience had been identified as a locus of revelation.

Gaudium et spes encourages dialogue within the Church, between members of the Church and others, between believers and non-believers, and between the Church and the world.

It was in response to these as well as to the *Decree on the Pastoral Office of Bishops*, which states, 'Bishops should be especially concerned about catechetical instruction ... They should furthermore ensure that catechists are adequately prepared for their task, being well instructed in the doctrine of the Church, and possessing both a practical and theoretical knowledge of the laws of psychology and educational method'[11], that the *General Catechetical Directory* was published by the Sacred Congregation for the Clergy in 1971. The specific origins of the Directory are in paragraph 44 of the Decree, which calls for 'a directory for the catechetical instruction of the Christian people in which the fundamental principles of this instruction and its organisation will be dealt with and the presentation of the books relating to it'. In its foreword it is stated that the Directory was intended for: 'Bishops, Conferences of Bishops and all who under their leadership and direction have responsibility in the catechetical field. The immediate purpose of the Directory is to provide assistance in the production of catechetical directories and catechisms.'[12] It was also stated that 'the specific task of applying the principles and declarations contained in this Directory to concrete situations properly belongs to the various episcopates, and to do this by means of national and regional directories and by means of catechisms and the other aids which are suitable for effectively promoting the ministry of the word'.[13] The *General Catechetical Directory* then, was a text which, in order to be properly useful in a particular country, needed to be adapted, taking into account the particular historical and cultural context, a task which until recently was not attended to in Ireland.

The Irish Bishops' Conference responded to the new understandings of catechetical methodologies in a number of catechetical initiatives. A new syllabus for religious education at post primary level was written in 1966. There was, however, some dissatisfaction with it. At their meeting in Maynooth in 1969, the Bishops' Conference decided that a new syllabus, leading to a new series of textbooks for use in Irish secondary schools north and south of the border, should be created.

I believe that this was a most significant move in Irish catechetical development and was in fact the breaker of new ground out of which other initiatives grew. The situation at that time regarding religious education in Irish post primary schools was summed up by Bishop Cahal Daly. Bishop Daly, at the time the chairman of The Irish Catholic Bishops' Commission on Catechetics, is one of the most significant voices in the recent history of religious education in Ireland. At a time when new ground was being broken in the area of religious education, strong leadership was required from someone who understood the issues and was prepared to take them on board even if they proved unpopular in some areas. He said:

> Up to 1966, scripture, doctrine, apologetics, Church history and Liturgy were taught separately. This compartmentalised programme was artificial, abstract and remote from the life of young Christians. The new syllabus of 1966 set out to integrate these various studies in one unified course and thus bring the teaching of religion closer to life and to faith as lived. It helped to achieve this. However, in many cases the teacher was not equipped to integrate scripture, doctrine, Church history etc. in one coherent course. As they had been taught,

apologetics, scripture etc. had each its own sequence. The teacher knew where he was going. The 1966 course seemed to lack this thread of continuity and contributed to a good deal of confusion. New theological thinking and changed attitudes among adolescents as a consequence of general culture change further complicated the situation. The revision of the syllabus now in progress has to confront these difficulties ... First the syllabus will seek to break with the 'creed-cult-code' structure of the first three courses of the 1966 syllabus ... The second task will be to arrange the syllabus in such a manner that teachers will see how to integrate apologetics, Church history, liturgy etc. where relevant ... A catechetical theme outlines doctrine but it also looks to the pupil to see the needs, experiences and situations in his life to which this teaching gives meaning. The catechetical theme is concerned with revelation – with an aspect of God's message and God's work for someone. A syllabus can only outline this in a general way. The teacher will have to work out how the theme fits the life situations of his pupils whether in a rural area or an urban area, Belfast or Cork and in whatever type of school. To help him with this the new syllabus will be worked out in a special teacher's book as well as in the book for pupils. Formerly it was customary to speak of catechising as if it mainly involved teaching a list of doctrines. Today it is more emphasised that other things are also involved – the relationships established between teachers and pupils, between one pupil and another, the life of the faithful and service or prayer which the pupil is inspired to undertake. That is why teachers need a fairly well-developed syllabus which will be a guide to more than doctrinal content. They need guidelines as to method and approach – what some specialists call process content. It is above all in the process of catechising that attitudes are fostered. They are fundamental in religious education but it is difficult to cater for them in a content syllabus. That is the reason for having a special teachers book.[14]

What we have here is actually an articulation of a philosophy of religious education which has been normative in all catechetical development in Ireland since then. It offered an understanding of religious education as a discipline in its own right: not theology, not scripture and not education but informed by each of these. The provision of a teacher text, outlining methodologies and providing background information for the teacher, as well as a pupil book, is a strategy that has been used in many catechetical publications through the years. Later in the same article, Bishop Daly calls for specialist religion teachers, 'Schools need now more specialised religion teachers to help co-ordinate and direct the work of the various religion teachers on the staff ... Some system of sponsorship will have to be devised to encourage more teachers to specialise in religion.'[15]

Already there were two institutes in Ireland which specialised in training religious educators. The early pioneers in the post Vatican catechetical renewal studied *in Lumen Vitae Institute* in Brussels, *Corpus Christi* in London or in the United States. However, Mater Dei Institute was founded in 1966, under the patronage of the Archbishop of Dublin. Mater Dei has been a significant voice in religious education, through the contribution of its graduates and through the publications and research of its staff. It has responded to the changing needs of the times by pioneering the professional training of school chaplains, by promoting critical reflection and research in the areas of Religion and Education, and Religion and Culture. In 2002 a new undergraduate Batchelor of Arts degree in Irish Studies and Religious Studies was introduced. The Institute can also award the M.A. and Ph.D. for research. In 1999 Mater Dei became a college of Dublin City University. Today the Institute states in its strategic plan: 'The Institute is an important site where Christianity can negotiate openly with a plurality of other cultures, attitudes and systems of belief and no belief, and advocates the necessity of this negotiation by inviting people of all persuasions to participate in it.'

Another significant voice is that of Mount Oliver Institute of Religious Education, which was founded in 1969. At that time the diocesan advisors in Northern Ireland began to lobby the Northern Bishops with the idea that an institute for catechetical research and education would be established in the northern part of the country. In October 1968 Cardinal Conway approached Fr Bobby McKenna to ask him if he would be the first director of the new institute to be established in the convent of the Franciscan Sisters in Dundalk, a portion of which was rented from the sisters to become the institute. Staff were recruited and the institute opened its doors to the first group of 46, mostly Irish, students in September 1969. In his address at the opening of the Institute, Cardinal Conway said:

> The work of this institute will be right at the centre of the Church's first activity on earth. There are many offices in the Church of an administrative nature for example, of which it may be difficult to see at first

glance the connection with the preaching of the gospel or the transmission of the life of grace. Not so with the work of this Institute. Here you shall be immediately and directly concerned with the handing on of faith.[16]

Mount Oliver Institute continued to provide post-graduate training for students interested in becoming involved in religious education at primary, post primary or adult level until 1991. Prior to the opening of Mount Oliver, while Mater Dei provided training in the main at that time for students interested in teaching in second-level schools, there was no place in Ireland which offered specialised training for someone who wished to study religious education with an emphasis on either primary or adult education. After the closure of Mount Oliver there was once again no facility for primary teachers to do post-graduate studies in religious education with an emphasis on primary education until, following an initiative from Veritas, the MA in Religious Education Primary was commenced, jointly sponsored by Mater Dei Institute and St Patrick's College of Education. During its lifetime Mount Oliver had in its student body students from Kenya, Nigeria, the Philippines, India, Australia, the USA, New Zealand and the UK. In fact the international nature of the student body was one of its particular characteristics.

The new catechetical materials, which emerged from the 1969 revision of the syllabus for use in Irish post primary schools at Junior Cycle level, came in three titles: *Christ With Us*, *Saved In Christ*, *United In Christ*, written by Genevieve Mooney, John Heneghan and Macartan McQuaid and published between 1972 and 1974.

In the foreword to the third title in the series, Bishop Cahal Daly, then chairman of the Episcopal Commission on

Catechetics, describes the thematic approach which is used as a way of presenting doctrine so that, 'it is seen by the young people as relating to the experience of life which they are currently undergoing, the difficulties which they are now experiencing, the questions they are now asking, the aspirations by which they are being moved, at this particular stage in their development'. Going on to argue against the once held belief that the catechism doctrine which was learnt in the classroom would be retained and would later be seen as relating to life he said: 'There is good pedagogical reason for saying that what is not seen as relating to experience at the time of teaching is not in fact assimilated or effectively learned at all, and therefore will not be likely to be retained or to be ever related to later experience.'[17]

Already there was an awareness that religious education could best achieve its objectives when home, school and parish worked in partnership. The authors writing at the time of publication of the second book in the series say: 'It is highly desirable that priests involved in parish work should be familiar with the content, method and approach of these new books. In preparing them the writers have made frequent suggestions for linking up what is being studied in school with the everyday life of the home and the parish.'[18]

However, time has made it obvious that the awareness that has been written in to many of the religious education textbooks has not necessarily translated into effective collaboration between home, school and parish. As work progressed on the series for Junior Cycle, a team was appointed to write a follow on series for Senior Cycle. Nano Brennan, Desmond Forristal, John Heneghan and Dermot Lane commenced work on a series which was titled *The God and Man* series. Initially it was proposed that the series would consist of eight titles, though all eight titles did not emerge.

- The Mystery of God
- Jesus of Nazareth
- Church and Worship
- The Moral Life
- The Christian in Society
- Approach to Scripture
- The Christian Heritage
- Makers of Modern Thought

It is interesting to note that on considering these titles it is obvious that they are reflected in a number of the sections on the present Leaving Certificate syllabus. The first title in the series was published in 1976. The series was represented by Sr Brid Greville during the 1980s, while the original series for Junior Cycle was replaced by *The Christian Way* series written by Fr Ray Brady and published between 1980 and 1982. In the foreword to the first title in the Christian Way series, Bishop Cahal Daly says: 'The first texts and materials were breaking totally new ground in Ireland, and they did so with outstanding success. No Catechetical text is ever the last or the only word. But the first word is often the more difficult to speak and the more creative in its effects. However, a need has long been felt for an alternative version.'

A hallmark of religious education at school level in both the primary and post primary sectors has been the willingness of the Bishops' Commission for Catechetics to take on board and respond to cultural and educational changes by producing new resources.

There were many publications during the 1970s and 1980s which impacted on peoples' understanding of the nature of the work of religious education. I will refer to just two, one written in Ireland and the other in the States.

Firstly, in 1980, *Christian Religious Education* by Tom Groome was published by Harper and Row. In an approach which he calls "Shared Christian Praxis", Tom Groome argues for the need to connect theory and practice, faith and action, and tradition and transformation. He outlines the shared Christian praxis approach in five movements. Though the approach outlined by Groome may not have been followed in its entirety in any religious education text which was published in Ireland, his assertion that while religious education was about faithfully handing on the tradition it was also about enabling students to work for the transformation of the world, influenced the approach taken by those who were creating text books at that time.[19]

Secondly, in 1981 the first edition of *The Experience of God: An Invitation to do Theology* by Dermot Lane was published by Veritas. In the introduction Dermot Lane describes the book as an invitation to:

> [E]xplore the religious dimension of human experience, to discover in faith the reality of God co-present in human experience, to situate the gracious revelation of God to man within human experience, to ground the activity of faith as a response to the experience of God and to live life more fully by participating passionately in the revelatory orientation of human experience.[20]

For writers of religious education text books or students, this publication, I believe, was and continues to be a core text, with the most recent edition published by Veritas in 2003.

In 1973, the Irish Bishops appointed a team of three writers to, in the first instance, write a syllabus for religious education in Catholic primary schools in Ireland and, based on that, to write a national catechetical series. The three writers were Bill Murphy, Kathleen Glennon and Sean McEntee. In its preparation the writers developed a system of consultation and piloting which has been the hallmark of all subsequent re-presentations of the series, and which led Bishop Cahal Daly to remark at its publication 'An unusual merit of the material is that it is not just a matter of theorists telling teachers; it is a distillation of the ways in which gifted and successful teachers do in fact teach.'[21]

In the introduction to the syllabus, catechesis is understood as 'the communication of Christian revelation to man in his concrete situation with a view to fostering faith'.[22] The same introduction acknowledges the difficulty of drawing up a syllabus at that time as follows: 'the chief difficulty of drawing up a syllabus at the present time arises from the existence of widely different conceptions of the nature of catechesis as well as of its aim, content and sources'.[23]

The syllabus goes on to outline the three catechetical methodologies, Dogmatic, Kerygmatic and Anthropological, and to stress that each approach highlights an important concern of catechesis. It says:

> Despite the extent to which they differ, these three approaches pursue the same ultimate aim, to lead the children to a deeper Christian faith. However they emphasise different aspects of faith; assent to truths revealed by God, commitment to God light on man's life or service to other men and the world ... Each of these approaches underlines an important concern of catechesis: fidelity to the content of the Christian message, recourse to is privileged sources, relevance to man's life.[24]

It names the 'Two poles of catechesis' as 'The Christian message in its totality and the child's life'.[25]

The syllabus was approved by the Irish Bishops and the series which emerged, *The Children of God*, was published between 1976 and 1978. The methodology based on the integration of the three approaches is the hallmark of all subsequent representations of *The Children of God* series.

As well as taking account of the latest developments in theological and catechetical thinking, the new series also sought to work with the latest insights from educational and developmental theorists. The new Primary School Curriculum was published in 1971 and the writers of *The Children of God* series were aware of the need to synchronise the approach and methodologies in religious education with those which were being used in other areas of the curriculum. The hallmark of the new Primary School Curriculum of 1971 was the movement from a curriculum-centred style of education to a child-centred style. In a chapter entitled 'The Changing Role of the Primary School' it states: 'Education was curriculum-centred rather than child-centred, and the teacher's function, in many cases, was that of a medium through whom information was merely transferred to his pupils.' Going on to outline what the changed emphasis would involve:

> Children now play a much more active role in their own education and consequently show much more self reliance, confidence and flexibility of mind in tackling fresh challenges when these are presented to them. The basic skills are achieved not so much through class teaching as through group activity, each child progressing at his own natural rate, being allowed full scope to express his own personality and experience the joy of discovery, each being

encouraged to consult a variety of appropriate reading material to ensure the extension of his horizons and the enrichment of his personality.[26]

The Children of God series was an audio–visual presentation. Each teacher's kit contained audio tapes and full-colour posters as well as teacher and pupil texts. During the 1970s and 1980s there was an air of excitement, enthusiasm and possibility among those working in the area of Religious Education. I am sure that this was, on the one hand, due to the investment which was being put into the area, in terms of personnel, time, financial resources and specialist expertise, and, on the other hand, to the general optimistic air which prevailed after Vatican II. Those involved in religious education seemed to believe that they were involved in something worthwhile, something that could and would make a difference. Possibility seemed to be in the air. It was a time when on Saturdays here in Mater Dei both sides of the lecture theatre would be full of people involved in religious education who had come to hear people such as Tom Groome, whose Irishness as well as his catechetical expertise added to his popularity, or John Shea, whose storytelling entertained, provoked and sent his listeners away energised and convinced that the Christian story was worth telling.

These events were organised by the Catechetical Association of Ireland, an organisation which brought together people involved in religious education from all over the country. A number of dioceses also set up what they termed Religion Teachers Associations, which met regularly with the aim of providing ongoing education for religion teachers. While some of those who made up the membership of the Religion Teachers Associations were trained catechists, many were not. For these the courses provided by the associations were the only sources of preparation or back up for the work they did in the classroom. In some cases, these associations also organised summer schools, which provided the opportunity for people to hear internationally renowned speakers in the area of religious education or other areas of relevance. One person who worked as diocesan advisor in the Diocese of Cork at that time spoke of up to 250 teachers attending a week-long summer school where the main speaker was Jack Dominion.

At the same time catechetics and those involved aroused no small measure of suspicion and apprehension. Were the students getting enough content? Would they 'know their faith'? Was it all too 'airy-fairy'? Was it in fact simply environmental studies posing as religious education? When I was speaking to different people about this lecture, one person speaking about the suspicion which existed in relation to catechetics and those involved said that in the 1970s if a priest was seen to wear an anorak, have side burns and become involved in catechetics, fears for his priesthood began to surface in certain quarters.

At the level of adult Religious Education, this was the era of the Maynooth diploma courses which were held in venues all around the country. These were two-year programmes, usually organised by diocesan advisors. They were attended by up to 100 people in each venue and were a sign of the appetite people had at that time to learn more about the latest thinking in theology scripture or liturgy.

The Rite of Christian Initiation of Adults was published in 1971. This document restores the original emphasis on the preparation of catechumens as a journey through various stages of initiation leading to the celebration of Baptism, Confirmation and Eucharist. It restores the original order of the sacraments. Emphasis is placed on the candidate's commitment to live the Christian life and their readiness for initiation is judged according to their ability to bear witness to the faith, practice love of neighbour and self-denial and turn to God in prayer. In the 1970s and 1980s this rite was seen as having little practical relevance in a context where infant baptism was the norm. However, in 1986 Breige O'Hare used the insights of the Rite of Christian Initiation of Adults as the basis for the Faith Friend Programme for Confirmation. The introduction states: 'the only authentic context for the Sacrament of Confirmation is a total ecclesial one, the context of integration into the everyday life of the Christian community'.[27] This and its companion programme for First Holy Communion provided a process wherein the candidates for the sacraments are accompanied on their journey of preparation by adult members of the community.

In 1975 *Evangeli nuntiandi*, the apostolic exhortation of Pope Paul VI, places catechesis in the context of evangelisation. Evangelisation was an important theme of the papacy of Pope Paul VI, as it was in the deliberations of Vatican II. He took the title Paul in honour of Paul, the apostle to the gentiles, and during his papacy he journeyed to distant continents on missions of evangelisation. For him evangelisation was 'The essential mission of the Church'.[28] Evangelisation is described as 'transforming humanity from within and making it new ... always taking the person as one's starting point and always coming back to the relationships of people among themselves and with God'. The importance of community and witness are also emphasised.[29]

In 1977, the synod of bishops met on the theme 'Catechesis in our time with special reference to the catechesis of children'. Two documents emerged: *Message to the People of God* and *Catechesi tradendae*. At the heart of catechesis the synod placed the Person of Jesus of Nazareth, the Way, the Truth and the Life. A link is established between catechesis and evangelisation while distinguishing between the two. *Catechesi tradendae* states:

> Let us first of all recall that there is no separation or opposition between catechesis and evangelisation. Nor can the two simply be identified with one another ... Evangelisation is a rich, complex and dynamic reality made up of elements or one could say moments, that are essential and different from each other ... Catechesis is one of these moments.[30]

The document goes on to identify evangelisation with the initial conversion, proclamation of the Gospel, and catechesis with 'the two-fold objective of maturing the initial faith and of educating the true disciple of Christ by means of a deeper and more systematic knowledge of the person and the message of Jesus Christ'. The document deals with the content of catechesis, the methodology for its communication and the responsibility for its communication.

One of the strong themes which *Evangeli nuntiandi* and *Catechesi tradendae* have in common is a strong emphasis on the role of the community.

The centrality of the family is also given prominence. *Catechesi tradendae* states: 'The family's catechetical activity has a special character which is in a sense irreplaceable ... Family catechesis therefore precedes, accompanies and enriches all other forms of catechesis'.[31] In 1980, the Irish Bishops published a pastoral letter entitled, *Handing On Faith in the Home*. As its title suggests, it emphasised the central role of the family in the task of handing on faith to children.

We in Ireland must never imagine that parents do not need to teach religion because we have Catholic schools to do that for them. Let parents never imagine that they have fulfilled their whole duty as Catholic parents by sending their children to Catholic schools. We do have good Catholic schools, perhaps the best that can be found anywhere, but the very best Catholic schools can never replace religion in the home.

This view was later reiterated in the *General Directory for Catechesis*, published in 1997: 'In a certain sense, nothing replaces family catechesis, especially for its positive and receptive environment, for the example of adults, and for the first explicit experience of the practice of the faith.'[32]

In 1982, following the publication of *Evangeli nuntiandi* and *Catechesi tradendae*, and in view of the time which had elapsed since the *Children of God* series was first published, a writer was appointed to commence work on a re-presentation of the *Children of God* series. The term 're-presentation' was carefully chosen. The content of the original series would not be changed. What would change were the methodologies and style of presentation. This re-presentation was completed between 1983 and 1987. Once again the emphasis was on the use of the most up-to-date methodologies and teaching strategies. The starting point was again the experience of the child and storytelling was central to the methodology.

Working from the same philosophy, *The Christian Way* series was re-presented between 1991 and 1993. As with the re-presentation of the primary school series, the starting point for this project was not to change the content but to change the presentation in light of the changing experience of the students for whom the material was intended and in light of new insights in the field of education.

During the 1970s and 1980s the social justice theme came to be seen as important in catechesis. Writing in 1986, Dermot Lane said:

> The transformation of the world requires the wisdom of the Christian tradition and the wisdom of the Christian tradition must be seen to lead to the work of transforming the world ... If the faith that religious education communicates does not lead to action for justice, then there is a real possibility that its message may become a self serving ideology.[33]

Many of the catechetical resources which were developed at this time contained a social justice element.

In 1992, the French Language version of the *Catechism of the Catholic Church* was published. The last authorised *Catechism of the Catholic Church* was published in 1566, just after the Council of Trent. Some of the delegates at Vatican II proposed a universal catechism but the notion did not get widespread support. At the 1974 synod Cardinal Karol Wojtyla once again proposed a universal catechism, but again it did not receive sufficient support. Again at the synod of 1977 there was a proposal that a universal catechism should be written, but once again it did not get support. However, at the synod of 1985, which celebrated the twentieth anniversary of Vatican II, a majority of bishops were in favour of producing a universal catechism or compendium of Catholic doctrine. The advent of the *Catechism of the Catholic Church* was initially a source of some concern to some catechists, who feared that it would bring about an unhelpful over-emphasis on doctrine in catechetical texts. However, the Apostolic Constitution, *Fidei Depositum*, describes the document as 'a reference text' for the entire Church,[34] 'a norm for teaching the faith ... a valid and legitimate instrument for teaching the faith' and again it states:

> This catechism is given to them that it may be a sure and authentic reference text for teaching Catholic doctrine and particularly for preparing local catechisms ... It is meant to encourage and assist in the writing of new local catechisms, which take into account various situations and cultures while carefully preserving the unity of faith and fidelity to Catholic doctrine.[35]

The Catechism acknowledges the importance of human experience in paragraph 33, when it says, 'With his openness to truth and beauty, his sense of moral goodness, his freedom and the voice of his conscience, with his longings for the infinite and for happiness, man questions himself about God's existence. In all this he discerns signs of his immortal soul.'[36]

Following the publication of the *Catechism of the Catholic Church*, the *General Catechetical Directory* was revised and in 1977, the *General Directory for Catechesis* was published. It defines its purpose in paragraph 11 when, in addressing bishops, Episcopal conferences and those with responsibility for catechesis it states, 'The immediate end of the Directory is to assist in the composition of catechetical directories'.[37]

Part One of the *General Directory for Catechesis* lists the fundamental tasks of catechesis, four of which correspond to the four parts of the *Catechism of the Catholic Church*: promoting knowledge of the faith, liturgical education, moral formation, teaching to pray. The other two are education for community life and missionary initiation.

Following the publication of *The Catechism of the Catholic Church* in 1992, the Catechetical Commission of the Irish Bishops' Conference decided that they should represent *The Children of God* series for a second time. This second representation is called *Alive-O* and it was published between 1996 and 2004, with a break of one year in 1998 to consider the implications of the publication of the *General Directory for Catechesis*. This second presentation had to take account of deep-seated social and cultural changes which had taken place since the previous presentation.

The 1990s were years of major change in Ireland. Following the high levels of unemployment and the new wave of emigration which bedevilled the 1980s, the 1990s were years of unprecedented economic growth. One of the first signals that the nineties was to be a new era in Irish history came with the election of Mary Robinson as president in 1990. Her mission was clear: to work for the elimination of inequality at home, to reach out to emigrants abroad and to immigrants and others who were marginalised at home. Her philosophy moved Irish people to a more mature and inclusive sense of Irish identity. In her inaugural speech she said, 'I shall rely to a large extent on symbols. But symbols are what unite and divide people. Symbols give us our identity, our self image, our way of explaining ourselves to others.' She was indicating that a reshaping of the meaning of being Irish would be central to her presidency.

The 1990s were also the years of the tribunals. Corruption was exposed in politics, in business and in the Church. By the end of 2000 there were six tribunals in session: the Flood Tribunal, the Moriarty Tribunal, the Laffoy Commission, the Lindsay Tribunal, the Baron Inquiry and the non-statutory Dunne Inquiry. Doubts were raised about the reliability of institutions which would heretofore have been seen as utterly reliable: the political institutions, the health service, the legal world and the Church. The resultant loss of confidence left a vacuum which impinged on peoples' attitude to the Church and anything it might teach. It was as if the layers of the onion were peeled away until there was no core. At the same time there was unprecedented growth in wealth, which gave people more opportunities and more choices than perhaps ever before.

In the 1990s, educationalists and organisational theorists were suggesting that language did not only describe reality but that the language we use does in fact shape reality. In a publication entitled *Locating the Energy for Change*, Charles Elliott says, 'It is the ability to communicate, to construct a shared set of interpretations, symbols and assumptions, expectations, moral codes and ways of exercising authority and accountability that make collaborative endeavour even in the simplest task possible.'[38] The 1990s were also the time when the interconnectedness of everything became inescapable. The change from a world view based on Newtonian physics to one based on quantum physics would change not only the way we thought about the world but the way we were challenged to live in it.

For those engaged in the preparation of religious education textbooks, all of these as well as the multi-cultural nature of Irish society, the changed nature of family life, changes in the patterns of religious observance, changes in the structure of the family and new educational insights, especially as presented in the new curriculum for primary schools, were all of significance.

One of the greatest challenges to educators in the 1990s was in relation to those who, from many other traditions both religious and cultural, and for a variety of reasons, had come to make their homes in Ireland. The challenge was to educate in such a way as to create, in the words of Mary Robinson, 'an attitude of mind that we are enriched in Ireland by those who come from other countries'.[39]

The distinguishing mark of *Alive-O* comes, I believe, from an understanding on the part of its authors that in catechesis it is difficult if not impossible to separate method and content. The methodology is therefore dictated by the content and the integrity of the content is dependent on the methodology. The *General Directory for Catechesis* states:

> The principle of fidelity to God and fidelity to man leads to an avoidance of any opposition, or artificial separation, or presumed neutrality between method and content. It affirms rather their necessary correlation and interaction ... A good catechetical method is a guarantee of fidelity to content.[40]

Working with that as starting point, in introducing children to the image of God as Potter, *Alive-O* provides for them to have the experience of working with clay. The activity of feeling the texture of clay, the opportunity to take clay in their hands and shape it, the sensation of having clay under their nails, the fun of seeing what they have shaped out of the clay will all become formative in their understanding of the content of the image of God as Potter. And there is only one way to teach children to pray: by engaging with them in praying, in such a way that the prayer activity becomes a space in which they experience themselves in relationship with God. *Alive-O* is an audio-visual programme using CD, DVD, posters, as well as pupil and teacher texts. *Alive-O* also takes seriously the need to forge links between the home, the school and the parish, by providing materials for parents in the form of newsletters and videos or DVD, and by providing parish links which aim to help the celebrant to make links during the Sunday liturgy, with the programme the children are doing in school.

Meantime at post primary level the long-discussed introduction of religious education as an examination subject was well on the way. As far back as 1978, the subject of religion as a Leaving Certificate subject was on the agenda for a meeting of the National Conference of Priests. Arguing against the introduction, Fr Seán Long, having labelled the examination system itself as suspect, goes on to say:

> It also seems to me that some teachers believe that an examination will interest the hitherto disinterested pupil. However, I greatly question the interest in religion thus achieved. Could it not be merely an interest arising from the need to gain more points in the Leaving Certificate? I can appreciate that an examination in religious studies would facilitate universities and other institutions that provide theology as a subject of course of studies. But is this not catering for the elite few who will pursue such a course while forgetting the primary purpose of religion class, which is to provide Christian formation for the pupils. Moreover, I do not think that it solves anything to make the examination optional. Such an action will give reason to those not taking the examination to become even less interested in religion class and perhaps to want to opt out altogether.[41]

Anne Looney, writing in 1996, compared the situation in relation to teaching religion in post primary school to the failed path of Irish language teaching in the past. She makes a plea for a more imaginative approach.[42]

Writing in 2000, on behalf of the Post Primary Diocesan Advisors, Fr Donal O'Neill welcomed the introduction of religion as an examination subject, while recognising the challenges it presents. He offered the following as advantages from the point of view of the catechist:

- A renewed sense of professionalism in their work
- Assessment will help foster more learning, help evaluate what has been achieved and improve motivation among students
- New resources and publications will become available
- Religious education will have an enhanced standing as an academically respectable discipline.

At a broader level he suggested the following as favourable outcomes of the introduction of the examination in religious education:

> It is important to demonstrate the idea that Christian theology is a serious intellectual pursuit which has contributed enormously to human culture and particularly to European culture. There is a need for higher academic standards and a greater level of knowledge about religious matters in the public arena. It is important to have a theologically literate society.

He also noted the challenges: the possible conflict between religion as an examination subject, with the demands it would make on a teacher's time, and catechesis; the possibility that when religion would enter into the culture of the points system, it would no longer provide the space for students to reflect. He did, however, assert that 'There is no conflict between the religious and intellectual work of the Christian school'. Interestingly, in the light of Cahal Daly's plea for trained religion teachers in 1971, he too laments the lack of adequate professional training in the area.[43]

The Intermediate Education Act of 1878 had forbidden the state examination of religious education. In anticipation of the repeal of this act, in the mid-1990s the NCCA established a course committee on religious education. As a result of the work of this committee, the NCCA published two syllabi, one for Junior Certificate, published in 2000, and one for Leaving Certificate, published in 2003.

This was against the backdrop of the curriculum and assessment policy outlined by the NCCA in 1993, which defines the aim of education as 'to contribute to the development of all aspects of the individual including aesthetic, creative, critical, cultural, emotional, intellectual, moral, physical, political, social; and spiritual development'.[44] This is envisaged in the document as the responsibility of the whole school. In 1985, the Government's White Paper, *Charting our Education Future*, said that by the end of Junior Cycle, students should, in accordance with their abilities, have 'formative experiences in moral, religious and spiritual education'.[45] Added to this the Education Act 1998 required schools to 'promote the moral, spiritual, social and personal development of students ... in consultation with their parents having regard for the characteristic spirit of the school'.[46]

While many were highly optimistic about the introduction of religion as an examination subject, there were also some misgivings, mostly based on a fear that the formational aspect of religious education would suffer as a result of the introduction of an academic dimension.

Writing in *The Furrow* in 2002, Tom Deenihan, diocesan advisor for the diocese of Cork, says:

> One of the compelling arguments for the introduction of an examinable syllabus in religious education was that such a development would increase the profile among pupils. It has! However, it must be remembered that this perceived increase in profile is linked to the introduction of an examination. Only religious education is examinable. The increase in profile is of no obvious benefit to non-examinable catechetics. The difficulty in this regard is that teachers, parents and pupils may adopt a utilitarian approach and become interested solely in the examinable curriculum. In that likely scenario, catechetics will be afforded even less time than at present, be regarded as not being of consequence and, in extreme cases, be objected to as it would take valuable time from an examinable syllabus.[47]

One factor which lent weight to the optimistic view was the fact that religion was already subject to state examination in Northern Ireland with positive results. Many felt that the introduction of the state examination would eliminate to some extent the apathy which was widespread among students and the frustration of catechists from their experience of teaching or studying a subject which was not for examination within a system which was geared towards preparing students to gain the maximum number of points. At a conference entitled The Future of Religion in Irish Education, in 1996, Kevin Williams said:

> I am optimistic that the introduction of religion as an examination subject will not lead to a neglect of the

non-examinable aspects of religious belief and practice. After all there are state examinations in religious education in Northern Ireland and it is unlikely that the catechetical formation of young people in the northern part of the island is inferior to that in the Republic.[48]

The Catholic Bishops' Conference took steps to minimise the concern over the perceived conflict between religion as an examination subject and catechesis. In 1998 The National Catechetical Office was established and Caroline Renehan was appointed as the first National Director for Catechetics. In 1999, the Episcopal Conference published guidelines for faith formation at Junior Cycle level, prepared by Caroline Renehan, which have as their aim to help teachers to see how the teaching of religious education as an examination subject can be successfully combined with faith development.[49]

Corresponding guidelines are at present being prepared to complement the Leaving Certificate Syllabus. The change to teaching religion as an examination subject, particularly at Leaving Certificate level, would pose some difficulties for teachers who were used to the non-examination system, especially those who were not trained catechists. To resource teachers during the change, the *Into the Classroom* series edited by Paddy and Eoin Cassidy was published by Veritas.

A series of textbooks, *Community of Faith*, *Community of Hope* and *Community of Love* for students at Junior Cycle level were written by Linda Quigley and published between 2001 and 2003. These take account of the requirements of both the Junior Certificate Syllabus and the Bishops' Guidelines for Faith Formation. Most recently, a series has been completed to meet the requirements of the Leaving Certificate syllabus for Religious Education and the Bishops' Guidelines for Faith Formation at Senior Cycle Level. The series, entitled *Faith Seeking Understanding*, was edited by Michael de Barra and the complete series will be ready for the school year commencing September 2006.

Other recent significant developments are the decision of the Episcopal Commission on Catechetics to appoint a team to write a national syllabus for religion education at primary level. This work is still in progress. The Commission has also seconded on a full-time basis Gareth Byrne to write a national catechetical directory for Ireland, thereby fulfilling one of the principal recommendations of the *Catechism of the Catholic Church* and of the *General Directory for Catechesis*. This document will provide the starting point for all future thinking in the area, and will be of particular assistance to those involved in the writing of new catechetical programmes.

In 2004, the NCCA, at the instigation of the Post Primary Diocesan Advisors, produced a framework document to assist those teaching religious education to Senior Cycle students who do not intend taking the subject in the examination. In it the purpose of the document is stated as follows: 'It offers teachers a structure within which to plan a programme of religious education for Senior Cycle. It is designed as a two-year framework, but can be extended to cover a three-year cycle if transition year is to be included.'[50] It offers considerably less detailed specification than the Leaving Certificate course, is shorter and offers more choice and scope for creativity for teachers and schools.

So where to from here? Of the many things which should be taken into account if we were to seriously apply ourselves to answering that question, I will talk about just a few. Religious education and catechesis must be resourced so that those involved are adequately trained and having been trained continue to be in-serviced so that they are in tune with up-to-the-minute developments. In a document entitled the *Situation of Catechesis in Ireland,* a report which was prepared for the Congregation for the Doctrine of the Faith and the Congregation for the Clergy in 2001, it was reported: 'Sadly there is a crisis at the moment in the provision of adequate professional religious education. Some suggest that less than 50% of all religious education teachers hold a specialist qualification to teach religion.'

The question of adult religious education obviously needs attention. The fact that the Bishops' Conference has established a Commission for Pastoral Renewal, with one of its briefs articulated as Faith Development and Family Life, with one person employed on a full-time basis is probably a step in the right direction. An unpublished survey carried out by the Bishops' Commission for Research and Development in 1999 found that most of what was happening in the area of adult religious education at the time was under the umbrella of Family Ministry, several dioceses had no one named with specific responsibility for adult education and there was a lack of appropriately qualified religious educators for adults. The recommendations of this report have as yet been largely unattended to and require attention.

Though there is a recognition of the need to forge links between home, school and parish, and though some initiatives have been taken in this direction, there is still an immense amount of work to be done.[51] In *Islands Apart: A Report on the Children of God Series* published in 2000, Martin Kennedy says:

- The classroom is a space of positive discourse and experience.

- The home is a space where there is little or no religious discourse and experience.
- The parish is a space of diminishing religious discourse and experience.
- The image of this is one of three islands, in some ways moving further apart, quite at variance with the theory of religious education as a partnership of home, school and parish.[52]

Writing in 1986, Una O'Neill said, 'One of our primary focuses for the future must be on one particular element that underlies the whole enterprise of Religious Education, that is the recovery of the symbolic imagination. The symbolic is the point of integration of life, experience, religion and as such it is intrinsic to the aims and objectives of religious education.' She goes on to say that the recovery of the symbolic has to take place at two levels: 'The first is the level of the experience of God, the second is the level of the meaning of that experience as expressed in the content of religion.'[53] I believe that this need to recover a sense of the symbolic in religious education is as urgent now as it was then.

Linked to this is the need to provide opportunities for participation in meaningful liturgies. Resources should be devoted to research in the areas of religious education and catechesis.

And lastly, I believe that religious education needs to be enriched by the arts. In his Letter to Artists in 1999, Pope John Paul II says, 'In order to communicate the message entrusted to us by Christ, the Church needs art.' He specifically mentions catechesis as one area of the Church's life which he feels would be enriched by art. The Letter specifically addresses itself to, and I quote, 'artists of the written and spoken word, of the theatre and music, of the plastic arts and the most recent technologies in the field of communication'. In its closing paragraph Pope John Paul quotes Dostoyevsky who said. 'Beauty will save the world.'

And I close with these words from the Letter which could provide a good pointer to the future for religious education, 'Beauty is a key to mystery and a call to transcendence. It is an invitation to savour life and to dream of the future.'

Notes

1. Edward Rogan, *Irish Catholicism: A Juridico-Historical Study of the Five Plenary Synods, 1850–1956*, Pontificia Universitas Gregoriana, Roma, 1987, p. xv.
2. Brendan Kennelly, *A Time for Voices*, Northumberland: Bloodaxe Books, 1990, p. 21.
3. Diarmaid Ferriter, *The Transformation of Ireland 1900–2000*, London: Profile Books, 2005, p. 570.
4. *Lumen gentium*, nn. 4-6.
5. *Sacrosanctum concilium*, n. 33.
6 . *Directory for Masses with Children*, n. 2
7. Ibid., n. 39.
8. Ibid., n. 17.
9. Ibid., n. 2.
10. Ibid., n. 6.
11. *Decree on the Pastoral Office of Bishops*, n. 14.
12. *General Catechetical Directory*, Sacred Congregation for the Clergy, foreword.
13. Ibid.
14. Bishop Cahal Daly, 'Bishops in Concert', *Intercom*, Nov 1971, Vol. 2, No. 11.
15. Ibid.
16. *Mount Oliver Magazine*, 1969–1990.
17. Genevieve Mooney, Macartan McQuaid and John Heneghan, *United In Christ*, Dublin: Veritas, 1974, pp. 11, 12.
18. Genevieve Money, John Heneghan and Macartan McQuaid, *Intercom*, Oct 1973, Vol. 4, n. 10

19. Tom Groome, *Shared Christian Praxis*, San Francisco: Harper and Row, 1980.
20. Dermot Lane, *The Experience of God: An Invitation to do Theology*, Dublin: Veritas, 1981, p. 3.
21. Cahal Daly, 'Becoming Children of God', *Intercom*, March 1976, Vol. 7, No. 3.
22. K. Glennon, B. Murphy and S. McEntee, *Catechetical Syllabus for Primary Schools*, p. ii.
23. Ibid.
24. Ibid.
25. Ibid., p. iv.
26. *Primary School Curriculum*, Dept of Education, 1971, p. 15.
27. Breige O'Hare, *A Training Manual for The Faith Friends Programme*, Dublin: Columba Press, 1986, p. 5.
28. *Evangeli nuntiandi*, n. 14.
29. Nn. 17, 20, 21, 23.
30. *Catechesi tradendae*, n. 18.
31. John Paul II, *Catechesi tradendae*, n. 68.
32. *The General Directory for Catechesis*, 1988, Dublin: Veritas, No. 178.
33. *Religious Education and the Future*, pp. 156, 157.
34. The *Catechism of the Catholic Church*, p. 3
35. Ibid., pp. 5, 6.
36. Ibid., n. 33, p. 16
37. *The General Directory for Catechesis*, n. 11, p. 17.
38. Charles Elliott, *Locating the Energy for Change*, Winnipeg: International Institute for Sustainable Development 1999, p. 15.
39. *The Irish Times* (9 March 1988) reporting on a major forum on human rights held in Dublin, March 1988.
40. *The General Directory for Catechesis*, Dublin: Veritas, 1998, No. 149.
41. 'RE in the Leaving?' *Intercom*, Vol. 9, Nos 7/8, July/August 1978.
42. *The Church in a New Ireland*, Dublin: Columba Press, 1996.
43. Fr Donal O'Neill, 'Religion as an Examination Subject', *Intercom*, February 2000.

44. NCCA, *A Programme for Reform: Curriculum and Assessment Policy Towards a New Century*, 1993, p. 26.
45. Government of Ireland, *Charting our Education Future*, Dublin: The Stationery Office, 1995, pp. 47, 48.
46. Government of Ireland, *Education Act 1998*, Dublin: The Stationery Office, 1995, p. 9(d).
47. Tom Deenihan, 'Religious Education and Religious Instruction: An Alternative Viewpoint', *The Furrow*, February 2002.
48. Kevin Williams, 'Religion in Irish Education: Recent Trends in Government Policy' in Padraig Hogan and Kevin Williams (eds), *The Future of Education in Irish Education*, Dublin: Veritas, 1997, p. 18.
49. Irish Catholic Bishops' Conference, *Guidelines for Faith Formation and Development of Catholic Students: Junior Certificate Religious Education Syllabus*, Dublin: Veritas, 1999.
50. NCCA Framework Document.
51. *Do this in Memory of Me* by Maeve Mahon and Martin Delaney is a parish-based perspective programme for First Holy Communion. The programme was designed in the first instance for use in the Dioceses of Kildare & Leighlin and Ossory, and was published in these two dioceses. Following its successful publishing, and when it became obvious to its authors that there was an interest in the programme in other dioceses around the country, it was published by Veritas in 2004. 'This programme encourages and challenges parents, grandparents and the parish community to become more actively involved in the sacramental journey as the children prepare for First Penance and First Communion.' (*Do this in Memory 2*, Foreword)
52. Martin Kennedy, *Islands Apart*, Dublin: Veritas, 2000.
53. Una O'Neill, 'Religious Education and the Future', in Dermot Lane (ed.), *Religious Education the Future*, Dublin: Columba Press, 1986.

Ecumenism Forty Years on – Are we Still in the Desert?

M. Cecily Boulding OP

We are clearly not yet in the Promised Land of full Christian unity; I think we are probably wading through the Jordan, and I mean *wading* – God has not miraculously parted the water for us!

The Decree of the Second Vatican Council, *Unitatis redintegratio/The Restoration of Unity among Christians*, mandated not only a major shift in ecclesiastical relations and practice but, more significantly, a fundamental revolution in the theology that informs that practice.

The *Introduction* to the Decree says, among other things, 'Certainly such divisions openly contradict the will of Christ ... in recent times he has begun to bestow more generously upon divided Christians remorse over their divisions and longing for unity. Everywhere large numbers have felt the impulse of this grace ... there increases from day to day a movement fostered by the grace of the Holy Spirit for the restoration of unity among all Christians ... the Council gladly notes all this ... it wishes to set before all Catholics guidelines, helps and methods by which they too can respond to this divine call.'

The first two chapters lay out 'Catholic Principles of Ecumenism', i.e. the basic doctrinal positions from which we start, chiefly the assertion that there is, and can be, only one church that (as had already been said in paragraph 8 of the *Dogmatic Constitution on the Church*) subsists in the Roman Catholic Church with its divinely instituted hierarchy.

The Decree continues, however, with the newly recognised insights of ecumenical theology: 'From the beginning rifts appeared ... which St Paul censures as damnable ... in subsequent centuries dissensions arose ... for which people on both sides were often to blame ...' Let us briefly recall those rifts. They occurred at three significant points in history:

In the fifth century groups of Christians who could not accept the statements of christological doctrine formulated by the councils of Ephesus and Chalcedon were separated from communion with Rome; we refer to them as the pre-Chalcedonian churches; they are mainly located in the near East.

In the eleventh century a permanent schism opened up between Rome and Constantinople, between the western Latin and the eastern Orthodox churches – churches in the plural because their patriarchates are autocephalous, literally 'self-headed', i.e. autonomous churches in communion with each other. These too have their main centres in Eastern Europe and the Near East, but since the seventeenth century the latter have planted congregations in many parts of the world, including Europe and the USA.

In the sixteenth century the Protestant Reformation split European Christendom into four main blocks – Roman Catholic, Lutheran, Calvinist and Anglican – and all these, including Roman Catholics, have continued to fragment and subdivide ever since.[1] The World Council of Churches currently counts more than 340 separate member churches.

The Council of Trent, meeting intermittently from 1545 to 1564, clearly and solemnly defined almost every aspect of the Catholic faith in conscious opposition to Reformation positions as well as those of earlier heresies. The explicit stance was that 'Heretics could not be saved unless they returned to the fold of Rome'.[2]

The Catholic Position before Vatican II

As warfare and active hostility gradually declined in many places in the eighteenth and nineteenth centuries – largely as the result of exhaustion – 'good faith', i.e. inculpable and invincible ignorance combined with good will among other Christians, came to be tacitly recognised. However, the official Catholic position was reiterated by the First Vatican Council in 1869, when Pius IX issued an invitation to the Protestant world to 'return to Catholic unity'. It was virtually ignored by all except the USA Presbyterian General Assembly, which expressed a polite but decided refusal.

The Roman Catholic attitude for the first half of the twentieth century was not much more favourable, though there were some signs of a thaw: Leo XIII, Pope from 1878–1903, who wrote and spoke frequently about the need and desire for Christian unity, dropped the terms 'heretic' and 'schismatic' in favour of '*dissidentes*', or used titles that others used of themselves, such as 'Lutheran' or 'Anglican'. In England this led to the happier phrase 'separated brethren'.

The official temperature dropped again in the early twentieth century in direct reaction to the developing ecumenical movement among other Christians, exemplified in the Edinburgh Missionary Conference of 1910 and the Lambeth Conference *Appeal to All Christians* of 1920.[3]

The mainly Anglican organisers of the *Faith and Order Conference* of 1927 (a follow-up to the 1910 Conference) sent a courteous invitation to Rome to participate; it was harshly rejected by Pope Pius XI, who accused them of 'indiscriminately inviting apostate Christians, infidels and the like'. His 1920 encyclical, *Mortalim Animos*, referred to the ecumenical movement as a 'most grave error' and warned of the dangers of 'indifferentism' and of the Catholic Faith being blurred or watered-down; the individual conversion of 'misguided Christians' to Rome was the only way to reunion. 'Pan-Christianity' was being established by mutual love to the disparagement of faith, whereas there could be no true unity without unity in faith.

In 1944 Pius XII's encyclical on *The Mystical Body of Christ* restated that:

> It is a dangerous error to hold that one can adhere to Christ as head of the Church without loyal allegiance to his vicar on earth. If the visible head is eliminated and the visible bonds of union broken, the mystical body of Christ is so obscured and disfigured that it becomes impossible for those seeking the harbour of salvation to see or discern it.

He invited everyone to yield to the inner stirrings of grace and strive to extricate themselves from that state in which they cannot be secure of their own salvation (para. 39). In 1948, with the long-delayed inauguration after the Second World War of the World Council of Churches, the same objections were repeated – a little more gently – as had been raised in 1928.

The first official crack in this position came in 1949 when the exaggerated assertions of the American Jesuit Leonard Feeney about 'outside the Church no salvation' forced the Holy Office in Rome to articulate a very carefully nuanced statement about the necessity, or otherwise, for salvation of explicit membership of the visible structured Catholic Church. This was significant not just for the dramatic row that blew up, but rather for evoking the first officially stated analysis of that question.[4]

Alongside this rigid official stance there had of course been other, more encouraging developments: commonly agreed seasons and occasions of prayer for Christian unity dated back to 1835 and received approval from Pope Leo XIII in 1897. Despite official prohibition, some Catholics, priests as well as laity, attended the 1927 and subsequent *Faith and Order* conferences and the WCC Assemblies after they were established. In 1936 the Abbey of Chevetonge in Belgium was established by the Benedictines to develop relations with other Christians in the East, and gradually widened its scope to include dissident Christians of the West.

Probably the most significant prelude to Vatican II was the publication in 1937 by the Dominican Yves Congar of his book, *Divided Christendom*,[5] a serious theological analysis of and comment on the ecumenical situation. At the time it earned him severe disapproval in Rome. This inhibited his teaching and preaching, but not his continued study of the topic, which was to provide a major impulse and directive for the work of Vatican II and effectively translated the 'reunionism' of Pius XII into 'ecumenism', which is something entirely different.[6]

Vatican II

Chapter 2 of the *Decree on Ecumenism* boldly proclaims that, 'Today, under the influence of the Holy Spirit, many efforts are being made in prayer, word and action to attain that fullness of unity which Jesus Christ desires. The Council exhorts all the Catholic faithful to recognise the signs of the times, and to take an active and intelligent part in the work of ecumenism' (n. 4). 'In ecumenical work, their primary duty is to make a careful and honest appraisal of whatever needs to be renewed and done in the Catholic household itself' (n. 5). 'Deficiencies in moral conduct or discipline, or even in the way that Church teaching has been formulated ... should be set right at the opportune moment and in the proper way' (n. 6). 'It is allowable, even desirable, that Catholics should join in prayer with their separated brethren' (n. 8). 'We must become familiar with the outlook of our separated brethren; study is absolutely required for this, pursued in fidelity to the truth and a spirit of good will' (n. 9).

'The manner and order in which Catholic belief is expressed should not become an obstacle to dialogue with our separate brethren. It is essential that it be clearly expressed in its entirety ... it must be explained more profoundly and precisely in such a way and such terms that our separated brethren can also really understand it ... In dialogue ... Catholic theologians should remember that in Catholic doctrine, there exists an order or hierarchy of truths since they vary in their relation to the foundations of Christian faith' (n. 11).

Pope Pius XI's 1928 concern about 'indifferentism' and 'watering-down the Catholic faith' have clearly receded into the background! It would seem difficult, too, to square Pius XII's 1944 position with the Decree's assertion that, 'Those properly baptised are put in some, though imperfect communion with the Catholic Church ... the Catholic Church accepts them with respect and affection as brothers .... Justified by faith in baptism, they are incorporated into Christ and have the right to be called Christians ... The separated churches and communities as such ... have by no means been deprived of significance and importance in the mystery of salvation for the Spirit of Christ has not refrained from using them as means of salvation' (n. 3).

Chapter 3 considers *The Churches and Ecclesial Communities Separated from the Roman Apostolic See.* The term 'ecclesial communities' was coined for two reasons: the council at the time was unable to produce a satisfactorily agreed definition of 'church', and certainly some of the bodies concerned would not wish to be designated 'churches' in the sense in which the Roman Catholic Church uses the word. The Council, however, could not and did not wish to deny the ecclesial character of groups which are clearly more than merely voluntary human associations, but freely admitted that an adequate description of them was a task too difficult to be attempted in the document.[7]

The chapter looks first at pre-Chalcedonian and Orthodox churches. It recognises their historic origins and the acceptability of differing developments in discipline, liturgy, spirituality and even the theological expression of doctrine. However, it admits that, in a context lacking in charity and mutual understanding, and complicated by extraneous political and social factors, such developments opened the way for real divisions. Since mutual recognition of valid sacraments has been preserved it hopes that dialogue, together with the principle of imposing no burden beyond the indispensable, might eventually lead to the healing of the East–West schism (nn. 14–18).

With regard to the churches and ecclesial communities of the West, the chapter recognises more weighty differences of a historical, sociological, psychological and cultural character, as well as in the interpretation of revealed truth. It offers considerations that could facilitate dialogue, noting some obvious points of contact with the Roman Catholic Church in doctrine, spirituality and sacramental practice.

The Decree ends by urging Catholics to abstain from 'frivolous or imprudent zeal'; their activity must be 'fully and sincerely Catholic ... loyal to the truth received from the Apostles and Fathers, in harmony with the faith which the Catholic Church has always professed, at the same time tending towards that fullness in which Our Lord wants his body to grow in the fullness of time.' It hopes that the initiatives of Catholics together with their separated brethren will go forward 'without obstructing divine providence, or prejudging the future inspirations of the Holy Spirit.' It recognises that the objective of the reconciliation of all Christians in the one and only church of Christ 'transcends human powers and gifts' (n. 24).

Where Are we Now?
That was forty years ago – so where are we now? On the theoretical, theological level, dialogue has led to considerable progress. Most notably: our common baptism is recognised as valid by the majority of Christian churches in these islands. Gone are the days of automatic conditional baptism for all converts; indeed we may no longer use that word for those who wish to be received into *full* communion with the Roman Catholic Church. The very restrictive conditions previously demanded for a mixed marriage have been extensively relaxed, precisely out of respect for the faith of the non-Catholic spouse and the sacred and – for us sacramental – nature of the marriage bond among Christians.

Some, albeit limited, extension has been made in the conditions under which non-Roman Catholic Christians may receive the Eucharist in a Catholic church. In 1999 an agreed understanding was achieved between the Roman Catholic Church and Lutheran World Federation on the doctrine of 'Justification by grace through faith' – the nub of the sixteenth century Reformation divide has been recognised as no longer a church-dividing issue.[8]

Roman Catholics have developed a much greater
appreciation of the theology, liturgy and spirituality of
other Christians, aptly expressed by Pope Paul VI at the
time of the canonisation of the Forty Martyrs of England
and Wales, when he asserted that there would be 'no
seeking to lessen the spiritual patrimony of the Anglican
Church when the Roman Catholic Church was finally able
to embrace again her ever-beloved sister'.[9]

Surveying the work of ARCIC from 1968 to 2000,
Cardinal Cormac Murphy-O'Connor of Westminster
pointed out that it is good to remember the common faith
we share: the scriptures, the creeds, traditions of liturgy and
spirituality; this constitutes a real *koinonia*/communion
which has its origin in the communion of the Trinity –
Father, Son and Holy Spirit.

A recent article by an English Catholic priest pointed out
that the German Protestant theologian, Oscar Cullman,
distinguished different rhythms in the history of salvation:
before Christ all things from creation onwards pointed to
Christ and converged on him. Now we live in 'salvation
time' – the salvation already won for us by Jesus Christ.
Though there is still a dimension of 'not yet' about our
personal salvation, we are already united with all
Christians, not only in our joyful hope, but in a salvation
already gained in principle which has united us all for two
thousand years.[10]

There have been advances in practice too: we do quite
often share liturgical as well as informal worship with other
Christians, though it may take some major event or disaster
to make us do it! Shared pastoral activity in the form of
joint chaplaincies in hospitals, prisons and airports is quite
common, at least in Britain. We now normally extend
mutual invitations not only to family events like weddings
and baptisms, but also to the installation of ministers,

priests and bishops. In England, there is a degree of cooperation in local church administration, with joint meetings and consultations among the local clergy. There is some shared instruction in the faith by way of joint RCIA and Alpha courses, and some schemes of joint education and training for ordinands. Church leaders also cooperate in the sphere of combined statements on topical and social questions.

The Issue of Ecclesiology

With this increasing level of cooperation why is a fully united church only a distant dream? I think the remaining theoretical difficulty lies in the area of ecclesiology. We may have reached agreement with some, if not most of our fellow Christians on key issues such as baptism, marriage, justification, even the Eucharist, but these still need to be located within the more fundamental framework of agreement on the nature of the Church.

Specifically there needs to be some agreed and satisfactory interpretation of the reality of plurality within the unity of the Church. The Dominican Jean Marie Tillard, a great ecumenist and rigorous theologian, indicated two essential factors as a starting point: the well springs of grace have clearly not dried up in spite of our divisions, and the barriers between us are not impermeable. Evidently, the walls of division do not reach up to heaven. So we have to find an understanding of Church that is true to our faith, yet takes account of the denominational situation.[11]

He suggested that dialogues should study carefully the 'qualification' of mutual differences, to assess whether they are really doctrinal differences or rather divergent understandings of the same doctrine. It was precisely this approach that made possible the Roman Catholic–Lutheran Agreement. The Anglican–Roman Catholic International

Commission (ARCIC) has tried to remind us that the Body of Christ cannot be reduced merely to the institutional church even though it requires this as its servant. The members sought for a richness of faith that, without diverging on essentials, might be actualised by a diversity of theological insights.[12] Others have begun to concentrate on the same theme.

An article by Joseph Fameree, Professor of Ecclesiology and Ecumenism at Louvain, entitled *Legitimate Diversity in the Roman Catholic Tradition*, was published in 2003.[13] The International Roman Catholic Methodist Dialogue is currently studying how each can recognise the existence of 'church' in the other, in preparation for their 2006 Report.[14]

One possible approach was indicated by Cardinal Willebrands when he was president of the Pontifical Council for Christian Unity, as long ago as 1970, when he proposed the concept of 'types', in the basic Greek sense of the word *TYPOS*, which connotes the fact that the same reality can be embodied in a varying collection of external characteristics. Thus there could be varying 'types' or *TYPOI* of the Christian faith, each marked by its own internal consistency in terms of theological and liturgical expression, Christian life, fellowship and discipline.[15] From the socio-psychological angle an unthinkable plurality may be generally more comfortable – live and let live – but as a doctrinal condition it is much less congenial to Roman Catholics. We have inherited and grown up with a theological tradition of clarity and exactitude governed by an iron logic that, if our position is right, those who differ from it must be wrong. We have, mostly, come to accept that unity is not the same as uniformity, but until we can really cope with the concept of plurality/diversity in unity, our progress will be slow, though perhaps easier for those less concerned with academic theology!

The 1996 *Joint Declaration* by Pope John Paul II and Archbishop George Carey of Canterbury recognised the continuing obstacles to reunion, but urged people to 'repent for the past – *metanoia* – a change of heart, a deliberate turning round – and open themselves to God's transforming power ...' Such repentance will surely have to include a conversion of mind which escapes from the sole domination of classical logic and Tridentine definition, and recognises that God *can* do a new thing (cf, I Sam. 3:11). Such a conversion actually takes generations and not just one lifetime. New insights cannot really bear fruit unless they are 'positively received' by the generality of folk, not just by the more penetrating or *avant garde* theologians.

Such reception is not merely a juridical act of obedience to legitimately constituted authority; it is the active giving of assent, following a process of judgement, by which an individual or the whole People of God as such receive as truth in the fullest sense of their faith the new insights offered. This is essential if any church tradition is to appropriate a truth that has not arisen out of or been previously perceived by that tradition, and recognise and adopt it as a legitimate formulation of the faith of the Apostles.

In such a process local churches and all the faithful are not passive or inert but exercise their God-given faculty of discernment. This of course presupposes an ecclesiology of *koinonia*, a perception of the Church as a communion of local churches or dioceses, 'in which and out of which the one, unique Catholic Church exists, as the Vatican II *Constitution on the Church* explained in its paragraph 23 following the teaching of the third century martyr Bishop St Cyprian'.[16] It presumes too a collegial concept of Episcopal teaching authority and a sense of the presence of the Holy Spirit. It is the church universal – the *sensus fidelium* – which is infallible in matters of faith. The consensus of the

Church and its reception of a given truth are the work of the Holy Spirit and the sign of his presence, a point cogently made by the English Bishops in their *Response* to *the Final Report of ARCIC I.*[17]

Though unity is an essential mark of the Church it is a quality always to be realised more fully – hence the use of that verb 'subsists' in the *Constitution on the Church*. The basic essential is always present in the Catholic Church as a quality it can never lose, but also as a quality to be evermore actualised and demonstrated, and the Catholic Church can no longer formulate its self-understanding in splendid isolation.[18]

This is a never-ending process because the Church is a dynamic living entity. Vatican II was able to embrace the ecumenical movement because of its renewed appreciation of the eschatological dimension of the Church: it saw the Church as God's people on the move, on pilgrimage between the 'already' and the 'not yet'. Ecumenical dialogue aimed at the ultimate visible unity of the Church requires not new doctrines but a new outlook, a new attitude, a real re-reception of the same old truths in an ever-changing context.[19] Real knowledge of the past is precisely the key that unlocks unexpected possibilities for the future, as was pointed out by Yves Congar.[20] Dialogue demands an attentive listening to what has been handed down from the beginning ... it enables us to remember forgotten aspects of Revelation, and to see in God's word possibilities we were not aware of or to which we had paid insufficient attention. Such a rediscovery of God's will as contained in Revelation and a re-evaluation of the origin of our divisions *is* taking place, but it demands our active re-reception.[21]

Notes

1. Roman Catholic examples: Old Catholics rejected condemnation of Jansenism 1713; further groups rejected definitions of First Vatican Council 1870; ditto Lusitanian Catholic Church 1880; Polish Independent Church 1914, etc.
2. Cardinal Sadoleto, *Letter to Geneva*, 1539
3. Lambeth Conference 1920, *Appeal to All Christians* on the basis of agreement on the four 'essentials' of Scriptures, Creeds, Two Dominical Sacraments, Historic Espiscopate locally adapted.
4. Holy Office, *Letter to the Archbishop of Boston* 1949: 'Christ commanded the Apostles to teach all nations whatever he had commanded ... included that we should be incorporated by baptism into the mystical body of Christ, which is the Church ... therefore no one will be saved who, knowing the Church divinely instituted by Christ, refuses to submit to the Church and the Roman Pontiff ... Our Saviour did not give a similar command that all nations should enter the Church, but established the Church as the means of salvation, without which salvation no one can enter the kingdom of heavenly glory ... The infinite mercy of God therefore, willed, not the intrinsic necessity of those divinely ordained aids to salvation, but the necessary end – salvation – to which they are designed to lead, for which only the wish or desire is, itself, absolutely necessary' (trans. and précis by present author).
5. English translation, M.A. Bousefield, *Divided Christendom: A Catholic Study of the Problem of Reunion*, London: G. Bles, 1939.
6. Cf, Yves Congar, *Mon Journal du Concile*, du Cerf, 2000, I, p. 19.
7. C.D.F, *Dominus Jesus*, Rome, 2000, n. 16: 'The churches which remain united to her [the R.C. Church] by ... apostolic succession and a valid eucharist, are true particular churches.'
8. Lutheran World Federation & the Roman Catholic Church, *Joint Declaration on the Doctrine of Justification*, 1999.

9. Cf, *One in Christ*, January 2004, Vol. 39/1.
10. Basil Loftus, *Rebuilding the Face of Christ*, in WYEC Unity Post Autumn 2004.
11. J.M.R.Tillard OP, unpublished paper written for Faith and Order Commission meeting, Mishi 1996.
12. Idem – 'Our Goal is full and visible communion', published v.s:n. 8.
13. Cf. *One in Christ*, October 2003, Vol. 38/3.
14. David Carter, 'Report: International Methodist – R.C. Dialogue Commission', *One in Christ*, April 2005, Vol. 40/2.
15. Sermon preached to the University of Cambridge, see *The Tablet*, 24 January 1970.
16. *Ep.* 55:24.
17. CF, Bishops' Conference of England and Wales, *Response to the Final Report of ARCIC I*: '...When the Commission declares "Although it is not through reception by the People of God that a definition first acquires authority, the assent of the faithful is the ultimate indication that the Church's authoritative decision in a matter of faith has been truly preserved from error by the Holy Spirit" (A.II.25) we believe that its thinking is compatible with Catholic teaching.'
18. Cf, Yves Congar, 'La Reception comme realité ecclesiologique' *Revue des Sciences et Theologiques,* 56 (1992), pp. 370–403.
19. Cf, Cardinal Walter Kasper, Presidential Opening Speech to the Vatican II Fortieth Anniversary Conference on *Unitatis Redintegratio,* Nov 2004.
20. Precise source untraced; quoted by William Henn, v. infra, n. 19.
21. William Henn OFMCap, 'The Vision of Unity Emerging under the Impact of Ecumenical Dialogue', in *Report of the Seventh Forum on Bilateral Dialogues,* WWC, Geneva, 1997.

Nostra aetate: Encountering other Religions, Enriching the Theological Imagination

Dermot A. Lane

The purpose of this paper is twofold: to examine the content of *Nostra aetate* and the theological challenges it poses for the self-understanding of Christianity today. This will require first of all an examination of the origin, the historical development of *Nostra aetate*, its relation to other documents and an outline of the reception of *Nostra aetate* in the post-conciliar period, with particular reference to the contribution of the late Pope John Paul II. In the second part of my paper, I will focus on the task of working out a theology about the positive relationship that can and should exist between Christianity and other religions. I can only do this from within the particularity of Christianity and hope that some affinities between Christianity and other religions will emerge. I do not seek, therefore, to develop a generic theology of religion, a one-size-fits-all account as it were, because that usually ends up giving us the lowest common denominator of other faiths, a dumbing down of differences and a bypassing of the uniqueness of each particular religion.

Part I: Background to *Nostra aetate*

When Pope John XXIII announced the convening of the Council in January 1959, it was not envisaged that a document dealing with the relationship of the Church to other religions would be issued. As one commentator put it, the publication of a document on non-Christian religions 'was an unexpected outcome of the conciliar process' and, as such, it arrived 'almost as an afterthought'.[1]

However, the relationship between Catholics and Jews, or, more accurately, the poor relationship between the Church and Judaism, was a matter of considerable concern to Angelo Giuseppe Roncalli. The horror of the Holocaust of six million Jews in Nazi Germany was deeply troubling for many Christians and the ongoing presence of so much anti-Semitism in Europe and beyond exercised the consciences of all churches.

Angelo Giuseppe Roncalli had been Apostolic Delegate in Turkey from 1935 to 1944. During that time, he sought actively to prevent the persecution and execution of many Jews. On becoming Pope John XXIII, Roncalli decreed in March 1959 that prayers for what at that time were known as the 'perfidious Jews' in the solemn intercessions on the Good Friday liturgy be deleted. In June 1960 he gave an audience to Jules Isaac, a French historian, who communicated his deep concern about the contempt of Jews found within Christian teaching. In September 1960 he requested Cardinal Bea to draw up a draft document on the relationship of the Catholic Church to the Jewish people for consideration at the forthcoming Council. In October 1960, he received in audience 130 US Jews whom he greeted warmly with the words: 'I am Joseph, your brother', words that deeply touched his audience at the time. In March 1962 while John XXIII was being driven along the Lungotevere in Rome he saw a group of Jews coming out of the synagogue; immediately he stood up in the car and offered them a blessing – an event that was subsequently described by a Jewish Rabbi who was there as 'perhaps the first real gesture of reconciliation'.[2]

In the meantime, preparatory work on a document on the Jews was progressing until in June 1962 it was announced in Israel, prematurely, that a Dr Chain Wardi would represent Jews at the forthcoming Council, without any consultation with the Vatican. This announcement provoked an outburst of protests from the Arab world against the Vatican. Discussions on the Jews came to a halt and the preparatory document, entitled *Decretum de Iudaeis*, was not presented at the first session of the Council in the autumn of 1962. Cardinal Bea, who was bitterly disappointed, made a passionate plea at the first session for the question of the Jews to be put back on the conciliar agenda. John XXIII readily agreed to this request. However, controversy continued to dog debate on the Jews:

- The play, *The Deputy*, was released on Broadway in January 1963, which, among other things, drew attention to the apparent silence of Pius XII in the face of the extermination of so many Jews;
- Strong reaction against a document on Jews came from the Arab world;
- Christian Arabs living in the middle east also objected;
- Why not just mention the Jews in the Constitution on the Church or put something into schema XIII or even *Dei verbum*?
- What about the other religions, especially Islam?

A second draft document entitled 'On the Attitude of Catholics toward Non-Christians and especially toward Jews' was presented in November 1963 as part of the decree on ecumenism but not debated. A further draft named 'On the Jews and Non-Christians' was presented and debated in September 1964. Though each draft document was controversial, there was a growing acceptance of the importance of making a statement on the Jews. Yves Congar, OP, however, remarked in his diary for September 1964, 'Anti-Semitism is not dead',[3] a comment provoked by the existence of a vocal group active both inside and outside the Council that were against any document on the Jews.

In spite of this ongoing nervousness concerning a statement on the Jews, a further revised text now called the 'Declaration on the Church's relation to Non-Christian Religions' was presented and discussed towards the end of the third session in November 1964 as a free-standing document. This later text was slightly modified and approved in October 1965 and promulgated on 28 October, with 2,312 in favour and 88 against. In the light of these controversies and the protracted birth of the document over three different sessions of the Council, *Nostra aetate* has been dubbed 'the declaration that almost did not happen'[4] and 'a miracle that it was ever passed'.[5]

Summary of *Nostra aetate*
The final declaration is made up of forty-one sentences and five different articles. This is the shortest document of the Council, but, arguably, the longest in implications for the church.

In article 1 it points out that all come from one and the same stock created by God and all share the same common destiny. People look to religion to try to resolve the riddles of life.

In article 2, it notes that throughout history there is found a certain awareness of a hidden power and even the recognition of a supreme being. Religions in general seek to answer the big questions of life. In particular, Hinduism explores the divine mystery and seeks to release people from the trials of life by ascetical practices, meditation and recourse to God. Buddhism testifies to the essential inadequacy of life in a changing world and therefore seeks to promotes liberation and illumination. This article concludes by saying that the 'Church rejects nothing of what is true and holy in these religions' and that these religions 'often reflect a ray of that truth that enlightens all men and women'.

In article 3, it points out that the 'Church has also a high regard for Muslims. They worship God ... who is one, living and subsistent, merciful and almighty Creator of heaven and earth who has spoken to humanity'. They 'submit themselves ... to the decrees of God and they link their faith to Abraham, they venerate Jesus as a prophet'; they 'honour Mary the virgin mother, and they await the day of judgement and the reward of God following the resurrection of the dead'. This article also acknowledges there have been controversies over the centuries between Christians and Muslims, urges mutual understanding and invites them to work together to promote peace, liberty, social justice and moral values.

Article 4, the longest, deals with Judaism. It recalls the 'Spiritual ties which link the people of the new covenant to the stock of Abraham' and 'acknowledges that in God's plan of salvation, the beginnings of its [Christian] faith and election are to be found in the patriarchs, Moses and the prophets'. The Declaration also points out that 'the pillars on which the Church stands, namely the Apostles, are Jewish, as were many of the early disciples'. It states that the Jews remain very dear to God since 'God does not take back the gifts he bestowed or the choice he made'. Further, the Declaration encourages mutual understanding and appreciation through biblical and theological enquiry and notes that 'neither all Jews indiscriminately ... nor Jews today, can be charged with crimes committed during' the Passion of Christ. Further, 'the Jews should not be spoken of as rejected or accursed as if this follows from Holy Scripture'. Finally it states unequivocally that the Church 'deplores all hatred, persecutions, displays of anti-Semitism levelled ... against the Jews'.

Article 5 concludes by saying there is no basis for any form of discrimination between individuals and that 'the Church reproves as foreign to the mind of Christ any discrimination or harassment on the basis of race, colour, or religion'.

Light on *Nostra aetate* from Other Documents at Vatican II
It should be remembered that during the many discussions leading up to *Nostra aetate*, it was suggested on several occasions that questions about the Jews and other religions might be inserted into other Council documents. Further, the 1985 Extraordinary Synod of Bishops meeting in Rome to commemorate the twentieth anniversary of the closure of the Council recommended that the interpretation of conciliar doctrine should consider documents in themselves and in their close relationship to each other so as to appreciate the full meaning of the Council's teaching.[6] Therefore, we must look briefly, at what other documents have to say, directly or indirectly, about the relationship of Christianity to the non-Christian religions.

Lumen gentium (November 1964) is regarded by many as one of the most important documents of the Council, principally because it lays down deep biblical and theological foundations affecting other documents, including *Nostra aetate*. For example, in article 13, the Council states that 'all are called by God's grace to salvation' – a clear statement about the universality of

God's offer of salvation to all through the gift of grace. Article 16 talks about those who have not yet accepted the Gospel but are nonetheless related to the people of God 'in various ways'. There are, first of all, the Jews and then come the Muslims who hold to the faith of Abraham and adore the one God. A third group are those who 'seek the unknown God'. Then come those who do not know Christ, but who seek God with a sincere heart and follow the dictates of their conscience. Lastly, there are those who, not without grace, seek to lead a good life. All of these, in one way or another, have the possibility of attaining salvation through the grace of God. Whatever is good and true among these groups is given by the God who enlightens all. The claim that the salvation of God is offered to these various groups begs the question: How is God's salvation communicated to these different groups?

The beginnings of an answer is given in *Gaudium et spes* (7 December 1965) which points out that 'the Spirit offers to all the possibility of being made partners, in a way known only to God, in the paschal mystery'.[7] Further, in article 41, the same document asserts, again, that the Spirit of God touches the lives of people, both in the past and in the present. Thus, this document on the Church in the modern world emphasises the active role of the Spirit in offering God's salvation to all.

In the decree on the Church's missionary activity, known as *Ad gentes* (7 December 1965), the Council picks up on the theme of the Spirit and points out that the Spirit was at work in the world before Christ[8] and says later on that the Spirit 'calls all ... to Christ and arouses ... the submission of faith by the seed of the Word and the preaching of the Gospel'.[9] This decree on the missionary activity of the Church also talks about 'elements of truth and grace ... found among people which are as it were a secret presence of God'[10] and refers to 'those seeds of the word which lie hidden' among other religions.[11]

These three documents provide a broad theological framework for understanding the positive relationship between the Church and other religions as outlined in *Nostra aetate*. In brief, the reason why the Church should reach out to other religions and engage in serious dialogue with them is because:

- All are called by God's grace to salvation (*LG* 13);
- The Spirit offers to all the possibility of being partners in the Paschal Mystery (*GS* 22);
- The Spirit of God was active in other religions before Christ (*AG* 4);
- The seeds of the Word are hidden in these religious traditions (*AG* 11);
- 'Elements of truth and grace' can be found in other religions (*AG* 9);
- Other religions 'often reflect a ray of that truth which enlightens all' (*NA* 2).

Evaluation of *Nostra aetate*

Looking back from the vantage point of forty years, the *Declaration on the Relation of the Church to Non-Christian Religions* is, in one sense, quite unremarkable, even bland from a theological point of view, and fairly flat in terms of what we today call inter-religious dialogue. Donald Nichol observes: 'It comes as something of a shock ... to notice how summary is its treatment of other religions apart from Judaism'.[12]

However, we must not read this document through the eyes of the twenty-first century. Instead, we must situate the document historically and culturally back in 1965. From that particular vantage point, it must be said in favour of *Nostra aetate*:

1. This is the first time that the Catholic Church reaches out positively to other non-Christian religions and this approach stands out in stark contrast to the traditional representation of religions prior to the Council.
2. This is also the first time that the Church explicitly deplores the persecution of the Jews and the presence of anti-Semitism, though it should be noted that Pius XI and Pius XII both had spoken out in favour of the Jews.
3. This is the first time the Church acknowledges that God does not take back his gifts and that all Jews, in the past or in the present, cannot be held responsible for the death of Christ.

How then are we to evaluate the historical and theological significance of this *Declaration on the Relationship of the Church to Non-Christian Religions*? On the positive side, it must be said that *Nostra aetate* 'represents a [major] watershed in the development of a theology of religions'.[13] Although a modest document, '*Nostra aetate* inaugurated a wide-ranging reappraisal within Catholicism of Christianity's relationship with Judaism'.[14] Further, *Nostra aetate* 'provided possibilities for dialogue between Jews and Christians that had never existed in the history of these two great religions'.[15] *Nostra aetate* ushered in a 'doctrinal revolution' and effected 'a radical upheaval in relation to the traditional representation of non-Christian religions'.[16] John Oesterreicher, one of the architects of the Declaration, describes it as 'a deeply theological' document.[17]

From a negative point of view, however, it must be pointed out that *Nostra aetate* remained silent on the question of whether other religions could be regarded as vehicles of salvation. In addition, it removed the word '*deicide*' from the final text; it failed to repudiate the atrocities inflicted on the Jews in Germany; it neglected to mention the *shoah*, the state of Israel and the post-biblical Jewish tradition. Further, *Nostra aetate* refused to spell out the theological implications of the Church's positive evaluation of non-Christian religions.

Nostra aetate, however, when read in conjunction with the other documents of the Council, marks a significant shift in the theological awareness of the Church. God is now understood to be active through the Spirit, through the seeds of the Word and through the gift of grace not only within Christianity, but also outside the Christian reality within other religions. While this new vision is present only in embryonic form in the Council and largely in documents other than *Nostra aetate*, nonetheless there is a significant shift, a theological reawakening, present at Vatican II which paves the way for major developments in the post-conciliar period.

The Reception of *Nostra aetate* in the Post-Conciliar Period
It would be impossible to summarise the many documents issued by the Church in its reception of *Nostra aetate* on other religions.[18] All we can do here is signal some significant stepping-stones employed in the construction of a new path in the Catholic Church's relationship with other religions since Vatican II

In the immediate aftermath of Vatican II, most activities focused on the other documents of the Council. Pope Paul VI, however, did give many addresses encouraging respect for and dialogue with other religions;[19] it should be remembered that in 1964 he wrote an important encyclical entitled *Ecclesiam Suam* and established, before *Nostra aetate* was completed, the Council for Dialogue with Non-Christians. Both of these in their time were significant stepping stones in facilitating a positive reception of *Nostra aetate*.

211

With the election of Karol Wojtyla as Pope John Paul II, the subject of inter-religious dialogue began to receive close attention. In his first encyclical, *Redemptor Hominis* (1979), he points out that the beliefs of non-Christians/other religions are an 'effect of the Spirit of truth operating outside the visible confines of the mystical body' of Christ in the world.[20] He notes that religions are a witness to 'the primacy of the spiritual' and are 'reflections of the one truth', 'Seeds of the Word'.[21]

In a later encyclical on the Holy Spirit entitled *Dominum et Vivificantem* (1986) there is an explicit emphasis on the importance of the role of the Spirit as a 'source of ... religious questioning' which influences the course of history, peoples, cultures and religions[22]. In the same encyclical he says, echoing *Ad gentes*, that the Spirit of God is active in the world before Christianity. Referring to the action of the Spirit in the world, he goes on to say: 'We cannot limit ourselves to the two thousand years since the birth of Christ. We need to go further back, to embrace the whole action of the Holy Spirit even before Christ ... from the beginning, throughout the world, especially in the economy of the Old Testament'[23].

In a subsequent encyclical on the missions, *Redemptoris Missio* (1990), John Paul talks once again about the presence and activity of the Spirit in the Church, in 'individuals ... society and history, peoples, cultures and religions'.[24] It is this same 'Spirit who sows the seeds of the Word ... who blows where He wills ... who holds all things together and leads us to broaden our vision'.[25] Further, there is recognition of the 'universal action of Spirit': 'we need to go further back to embrace the whole action of the Spirit even before Christ ... in every place and at every time ... in every individual'.[26]

A non-encyclical document coming from the Church during the pontificate of John Paul II entitled *Dialogue and*

Proclamation: Reflections and Orientations on Inter-Religious Dialogue and the Proclamation of the Gospel of Jesus Christ, was issued jointly by the Pontifical Council for Inter-Religious Dialogue and the Congregation for Evangelisation of People in May 1991, to commemorate the twenty-fifth anniversary of *Nostra aetate.* This document is regarded as the clearest expression of the Church's teaching on inter-religious dialogue. The primary purpose of *Dialogue and Proclamation* is to spell out the complementary relationship that exists between dialogue and proclamation. It suggests dialogue and proclamation, inter-religious dialogue and the proclamation of the Gospel, though not on the same level are authentic elements in the Church's evangelising mission; both are legitimate and necessary; both are intimately related but not interchangeable[27]. In brief, according to *Dialogue and Proclamation:*

> Interreligious dialogue is a part of the church's evangelising mission ... dialogue is not in opposition to the mission *ad gentes;* indeed it is has special links with that mission and is one of its expressions.[28]

Dialogue and Proclamation proposes four different kinds of dialogue:

1. There is the *dialogue of life,* where people seek to live in an open and neighbourly spirit, sharing their joys and sorrows, their human problems and preoccupations;[29]
2. There is also a *dialogue of action,* in which Christians and others work together for the development and liberation of people;
3. Then comes the *dialogue of theological exchange,* where specialists seek to deepen their understanding of their

213

respective religious heritages and appreciate each other's spiritual values;

4. Finally there is the *dialogue of religious experience*, where persons rooted in their own religious tradition share their spiritual riches in prayer and contemplation, faith and ways of searching for God.

These four forms of dialogue represent different ways of responding to *Nostra aetate*. This document, one of the most significant during the pontificate of John Paul II, also talks about 'the active presence of the Holy Spirit in the religious life of members of other religions' and states that 'all ... who are saved share, though differently ... in the mystery of salvation in Jesus Christ through the Spirit. The mystery of salvation reaches out to them ... through the invisible action of the Spirit of Christ'.[30] How? '[T]hrough the practice of what is good in their own religious traditions and by following the dictates of their conscience ...'[31] This document is one of the most explicit coming from the Church on the action of the Spirit in and through other religions offering them the possibility of salvation. One should note the increasing emphasis on the role of the Holy Spirit in Church documents, a point we will take up in part two of this paper.

One other document that must be mentioned is *Dominus Iesus*, issued by the Congregation for the Doctrine of the Faith in 2000, a document that sparked off controversy both within and without the Church. It seemed to call into question the progress of the previous thirty-five years. For many, the spirit of *Dominus Iesus* went against the positive orientation of Vatican II towards other religions: neglecting the real gains made in the post-conciliar church; omitting the special relationship between Christianity and Judaism; and drawing too sharp a distinction between theological faith and beliefs in other religions. On the other hand, it could be argued that *Dominus Iesus* provides a necessary and explicit articulation of the uniqueness of and universality of the Christ event, which, according to some, was being lost sight of in some inter-faith encounters.

It must be noted that, over and above these documents on the relationship of Christianity with the other religions, a series of other documents on the specific issue of Catholic–Jewish relations have also been issued since *Nostra aetate*. Again we can only mention these without going into any real detail.

The first follow-through on *Nostra aetate* dealing with the Jews specifically was the establishment by Pope Paul VI of the Commission for Relations with the Jews in 1974 and this Commission set about publishing in the 1974 *Guidelines and Suggestions for Implementing the Conciliar Declaration* Nostra aetate. These Guidelines summarised the themes outlined in *Nostra aetate* and presented them in a way that would promote better relationships between Jews and Catholics.[32] The Guidelines were followed up in 1985 by *Notes on the Correct Way to Present Jews and Judaism in Preaching and Catechesis in the Roman Catholic Church*. This document was intended to put into practice the developments contained in *Nostra aetate* and the 1974 Guidelines. The Notes are noteworthy for being very practical and for making reference for the first time in a Vatican document to the State of Israel and the extermination of Jews in Europe during 1935–1945.

The Notes were followed by another document in 1998 entitled *We Remember: A Reflection on the Shoah*.[33] This document, though widely welcomed, was criticised for distinguishing too sharply between Christian anti-Judaism and Nazi anti-semitism, and for making a distinction between the responsibility of the Church and the responsibility of individual Christians. A further document, issued in 2001 by the Pontifical Biblical Commission entitled *The Jewish People and their Sacred Scriptures in Christianity*, underlined the historical links and theological bonds between Judaism and Christianity.

Prophetic Gestures by John Paul II

While these documents are important benchmarks, there have been a number of symbolic and prophetic actions by John Paul II that perhaps speak louder than any documents. These include a visit by the Pope to the members of the Central Council for Jews in Germany in Mainz in 1980, during which he stated that the old covenant between Jews had never been revoked. This was followed by an historic visit to the synagogue in Rome in April 1986, the first visit ever made by a resident Pope in history to a synagogue. During this visit, John Paul II said that discrimination against Jews over the centuries was deplorable and he referred in particular to his abhorrence of the genocide visited upon Jews during the last war. This action was followed by a groundbreaking gathering of all religions in Assisi in 1986, which may turn out to be the most original and imaginative action promoting good relationships between all of the religions. This event was so significant that John Paul II felt it necessary to offer a theological justification for it at the annual pre-Christmas meeting of the Curia on the 22 December 1986. In that audience the Pope pointed out that Assisi was inspired by the radical unity of the human family founded on the doctrine of creation and the salvation of the human family in Christ. Further, Assisi was a visible expression of the teaching of the Second Vatican Council, especially as laid out in the decree on Ecumenism, the declaration on other religions and the dogmatic constitution on the Church. Thirdly, Assisi was a reminder that every authentic prayer is called for by the Holy Spirit who is mysteriously present in the heart of every human being.[34]

In the Jubilee Year 2000 there was a Mass of Pardon on the first Sunday of Lent during which Apologies were issued to seven different groups, including Jews. In this same Jubilee Year of 2000 John Paul II visited the Holy Land, with striking moments at Yah Vashem, the memorial in Jerusalem to the six million Jews who died in the Holocaust. In addition, there was during this visit to Jerusalem the placing of a prayer in a crack in the Western Wall, a gesture that deeply touched Jews and Christians alike throughout the world.

These significant documents and prophetic actions have highlighted, among other items, an important level of continuity between Judaism and Christianity. This continuity had been broken for the best part of two thousand years and now needs to be retrieved. By underlining the intrinsic relationship that exists for Christians with Jews, a number of important issues should be noted.

From now on, Christian identity and self-description must include explicit reference to Judaism. Christianity cannot be fully understood without formal reference to Judaism. This, of course, has far-reaching implications for the future of Christianity since, for the last two thousand years, Christians sought to understand themselves in isolation and separation from Judaism.

A further point is that there is growing agreement among Christian scholars that Christianity began as a reform movement within Judaism, and that for several decades, certainly up to the year 70CE and possibly into the second and even the third century also, Christians attended synagogues, observed Jewish feasts and followed Jewish customs.[35]

There is now a new awareness of the Jewish character of the whole of Christianity. This can be seen best in a new appreciation of the Jewishness of Jesus and his life, an appreciation that has important implications on the way we construct Christology. This new awareness of the Jewishness of Christianity now requires Christians to develop a post-supersessionist understanding of Christology, i.e. a Christology not over and against Judaism, not at the expense of Judaism but in a way that respects the originality and integrity of Judaism.

This in turn necessitates that care be taken if one persists in presenting Christianity as the fulfilment of Judaism. Classical fulfilment theories over the centuries have had a negative impact on the Christian perception of Judaism and need to be qualified now when used in reference to Jews in the light of *Nostra aetate* and subsequent documents from the Church.

A further requirement in the light of these developments is the need for Christians to develop what Johann Metz and others refer to as a post-Shoah theology, i.e. a Christology done not with our backs to the Shoah, but rather facing the Shoah.

Part II: Challenges Arising from *Nostra aetate*

In moving from the last forty years to the contemporary challenges, it becomes necessary to take account of the very different context in which questions about Christianity, other religions and inter-religious dialogue arise today. Context is all-important: it shapes the agenda, it influences the way we frame questions and it colours the response.

Religion has moved to the centre of the stage in the early years of the twenty-first century – but not always for the right reasons. Religion today is closely associated with terror and violence, especially in the light of 9/11/01 and what are now known as the bombings in Bali, Madrid and London (7/7/05). In addition, there was the publication of offending cartoons of the prophet Muhammad in February 2006 by the various newspapers in Europe, which provoked outbursts of protest and violence in the Islamic world. Ethnic unrest is a growing reality in many parts of Europe.

Alongside these developments there is also the rise of fundamentalism within Christianity, Judaism and Islam. From a secular point of view there is the promotion of what is termed tolerance towards all religions, but for tolerance, one should more often read indifference and apathy, inspired by the relativism of post-modern culture.

Furthermore, in Europe there are now new streams of successful secularism and unbridled capitalism, which are making it increasingly difficult to talk about religion and God in the public square. Taking transcendence seriously in Europe and engaging with the religious dimension of human experience is seen as socially and culturally problematic. This new cultural context in Western Europe has given rise to the privatisation of faith and raises serious questions about the possibility of God-talk in public life. Europe has lost its hold on God or God's presence has become less visible in European culture. The classical synthesis between God, cosmos and the human self has collapsed and so far nothing has replaced it. This new situation in Europe exists in striking contrast to the US, where religion and politics have become excessively intertwined. Is Europe the norm or the exception?

A further feature of the new context in which we find ourselves concerns the rise of multiculturalism across Europe, including Ireland. Multiculturalism has become the politically correct and acceptable response to the migration of diverse ethnic groups. However, events in the UK in terms of the London bombings in July 2005 and riots in France in the autumn of 2005, and the defiant publication of offending cartoons of the prophet Muhammad in the winter of 2006 suggest that multiculturalism may not be succeeding and may be giving rise to the creation of socially unhealthy ghettos. Multiculturalism is not about the assimilation of the minority by the majority; it is rather about cultural integration in a way that respects difference, acknowledges diversity and values otherness. What is needed in Europe and in Ireland are genuine intercultural exchanges and inter-religious dialogues that welcome and appreciate the human and religious other. Multiculturalism poses enormous challenges throughout Europe and there is no reason to think that Ireland is going to be an exception

An additional feature of the early part of the twenty-first century is the reality of globalisation, which is bringing the human family together like never before and at the same time highlighting the necessity for dialogue among the major religions.

In the light of this new context and the teaching of Vatican II, there is a growing conviction that Christians will be able to face this new situation more constructively and fruitfully in the company of Buddhist, Hindu, Jewish and Muslim friends, instead of facing them alone.

It is against this background and culturally changing context that I want to take up some aspects of the challenge of constructing a Christian theology of other religions.

While it is generally agreed that Vatican II was about ecclesiological reform, it is also true and perhaps more important to recognise that Vatican II and especially *Nostra aetate* was strictly speaking 'a theological event'.[36] *Nostra aetate* and the post-conciliar documents have effected a new theological awareness in the life of the Church. As seen, the Catholic Church now speaks positively about the seeds of the Word of God, the action of the Spirit of God, the secret presence of God, rays of the truth that enlighten all, and elements of truth and grace as present in varying degrees in other religions.

A new vision of God's providential relationship with all people is straining to come into view in various documents of the Council. This new vision requires a re-imagining of God's presence in the world, in other religions and in Christ Jesus. Vatican II, especially *Nostra aetate* and the theology of John Paul II, calls forth an enlargement of the theological imagination. This expansion of the theological imagination is one of the principal challenges emanating from the council. To be sure, the Council was about the church and liturgy, but it must also be emphasised it was about an enlargement of the theological imagination. This expansion of the theological imagination has been taking place over the last forty years in a variety of ways, but especially in understanding the role of the Spirit in the world, the nature of Revelation and the place of the person of Jesus Christ.

How are we to articulate a theology of the Spirit of God active before and after the Christ event? Both the Council and John Paul II talk about the universal action of the Spirit of God in the world in ways that push back the boundaries of the theological imagination.

Secondly, in *Nostra aetate*, there is a tilting towards a theology of general or universal revelation, when it talks about all human beings coming from the one God and sharing common destiny, that God's providential and saving designs extend to the whole of humanity, and that often a ray of the truth which enlightens all can be found in other religions.

A third aspect of Christianity, influenced by the enlargement of the theological imagination at Vatican II, is our understanding of the person of Jesus as the Christ in history. How do we express the connection between the universal action of the Spirit in the world and the particularity of the Christ event?

The question to be addressed is this: How are we to relate the new theological awareness of Vatican II and the expansion of the theological imagination this implies with the key issues of the Spirit of God, Revelation and the person of Christ? If we take seriously the thesis that Vatican II was 'a theological event', then we need to look again at our theologies of the Spirit, of Revelation and of Christ so that Christians can encounter the richness of other religious traditions.

God's Grace in the World as the Key to Inter-Religious Dialogue

A good place to initiate this reinterpretation of our theologies of the Spirit, Revelation and Christ is grace. A number of reasons suggest that a theology of grace is the proper point of departure for constructing a new theology of the Spirit, Revelation and Christ in the service of inter-religious dialogue.

The way we approach other religions is influenced, often unconsciously, by an underlying theology of grace. For example, those who espouse a dualist view of the relation between Nature and Grace usually end up with an exclusivist understanding of Christianity. In contrast, those who adopt an intrinsicist understanding of Nature and Grace veer towards an inclusivist theology of religions and within this inclusivism there are of course many variations.[37] A second reason for starting with grace is that one of the influences shaping Vatican II was what was known as *La Nouvelle Theologie* which prepared the way for the Council in the 1930s, 1940s and 1950s. This new theology had been worked out by people like Yves Congar,

Henri de Lubac and Marie-Dominique Chenu, all of whom sought to go beyond the extrinsicism of neo-scholastic theology in the early half of the twentieth century. In contrast to the manuals, all three sought to overcome the separation and dualism that had developed concerning Nature and Grace. All three brought Nature and Grace into a new (new at that time but old in terms of the patristic and medieval traditions) and intimate relationship, without conflating the two – even though all three differed on where they placed the emphasis.

This new theology of grace played a very significant role at the Council since all three were *periti*. For example, it was this theology of the intrinsic relationship between Nature and Grace that enabled the Council to charter a new relationship between the Church and the world (*GS*), between the Catholic Church and other Christian churches (*UR*), between the temporal and the eternal aspects of Christian faith (*GS*). More than anything else it was this theology of grace that enabled the Church to adopt a positive view of other religions in *Nostra aetate*, *Lumen gentium*, *Gaudium et spes* and *Ad gentes*.

· A third reason for beginning with grace is that John Oesterreicher, one of the main drafters of *Nostra aetate*, points out that it was a 'theology of the omnipresence of grace' that made *Nostra aetate* possible. Further, he notes this theology of the presence of God's grace as active throughout the world and among all nations mirrors the mind of the early patristic church.[38]

This influence of a new theology of grace can be found scattered throughout the Council documents. For our purposes here, it is sufficient to note the following striking statements. *Lumen gentium* asserts that: 'All are called to salvation by the grace of God'[39] and the same document goes on to state that those non-Christians who seek God with a sincere heart are 'moved by grace, to try ... to do his will as they know it through the dictates of their conscience'.[40] Likewise, *Gaudium et spes* talks about 'all people in whose heart grace is active invisibly'.[41] Further, the document *Ad gentes* on the missions explicitly speaks about 'those elements of Truth and Grace' in other religions, which it says are 'a secret presence of God'.[42] In a similar vein, John Paul II affirms that salvation in Christ is accessible to those outside the Church 'by virtue of a grace which ... enlightens them in a way ... accommodated to their spiritual and material situation'.[43] These few references highlight the underlying theological assumption of the universality of the grace of God in the world.

One of the theologians who has done most to develop a theology of the universality of God's grace in the world, and therefore in other religions, was Karl Rahner.[44] For Rahner, every human being comes into the world surrounded by the permanent offer of God's gracious presence and as a result there is in every human being what Rahner calls the 'supernatural existential'.[45] According to Rahner *all* are called to communion with God by grace and this universality of the grace of God touches and affects the ontological constitution of all human beings. Rahner describes this universality of God's grace in the world as transcendental and thus transcendental orientation reveals itself in the dynamic activities of human knowing, loving and acting. What this means in practice for inter-religious dialogue is that all participants in the dialogue have already been touched by God's universal saving grace, and this more than anything else should change the character of the relationship among all participants in dialogue.

Towards a Spirit-Centred Theology of Religions
We must now begin to see how this understanding of the

universality of God's grace in the world enlarges our theologies of the Spirit, Revelation and Christ. In this way, we can begin to move towards a theology of other religions that is able to transform the tired triad of exclusivism, inclusivism and pluralism, a typology that has outlived its initial usefulness because, among other things, it failed in practice to promote mutual understanding among the religions and to advance cooperation in areas of mutual interest.

As seen, one of the theological themes emphasised at Vatican II was the recognition of the action of the Spirit of God in the world and other religions. For example, the *Constitution on the Church in the Modern World* points out that the Spirit offers to all the possibility of being associated with the paschal mystery of Christ.[46] This embryonic emphasis of Vatican II on the Spirit is also found in the writings of John Paul II. For example, in *Redemptoris Missio* John Paul reminds us very explicitly that it has been a theology of the Spirit that has guided his own deliberations on the relationship of Christianity to other religions.[47]

It is surely instructive to note that two of the most influential theologians of the twentieth century, towards the end of their lives, came around to emphasising the need to give primacy to the Spirit within a theology of other religions. Paul Tillich (1886–1965), in the light of his encounter with other religions, wanted to rewrite his systematic theology around the Spirit and in doing so, he sought to present other religions as instances of a Spiritual Presence in the world. Tillich saw other religions as communities formed by the action of the Spirit and it was in this context that he presented Christianity as a religion of the concrete presence of the Spirit.[48] In a not dissimilar fashion, Karl Rahner (1904–1984), in the autumn of his life, also wanted to give primacy to the Spirit over Christ out of 'respect for all the major religions outside Christianity'.[49]

In the light of this new emphasis on the Holy Spirit at the Council, in the writings of John Paul II and among various theologians, I want to propose that a theology of the Spirit – Pneumatology – may be the more appropriate point of departure *in our time* for the construction of a theology of other religions and inter-religious dialogue.

To start with the Spirit is to begin with a theological symbol that is perhaps more recognisable and universally available to many of the major religions. For instance, it should be noted that the action of the Spirit in the world precedes the election of Israel, the advent of Christ and the revelation of the Trinity in the person of Christ. Further, from a historical point of view, and contrary to popular perception, the proper theological sequence within the historical unfolding of the doctrine of the Trinity is a movement from the Spirit to the person of Christ to God the Father. The Spirit of God has been active in the world, prior to the formation of the Judaeo-Christian tradition, and a historical case exists for arguing that the appropriate Trinitarian sequence is God the Spirit to God the Word Incarnate in Jesus to God the Father.[50]

Furthermore, by recognising the prior action of the Spirit in the world and other religions, we will be in a better position to see the Spirit as active in the life of Jesus and in the Christian community today. Within this Spirit-centred perspective we can begin to recognise all religions, including Christianity, as creative responses to the gift of God's Spirit poured out on humanity from the beginning of time.

All religions, in virtue of the outpouring of the Spirit, can be said to belong to one and the same spiritual family and are connected in varying degrees to the Spirit of God active in the world. All religions are Spirit-inspired and Spirit-driven. Failure by Christians to recognise the Spirit-gifted character of other religions will inevitably reduce their own capacity to appreciate Christianity as a particular and unique spiritual community shaped and formed by the personal Spirit of Jesus Christ.

In entering into dialogue with other religions, Christians need to remember that they are encountering others who have already been touched and gifted by the Spirit of God and that, therefore, there is a Spirit-shaped relationship among many religions. It is this unity in the Spirit that is the basis of respect, reverence and appreciation of the other. All human beings, in the light of this primacy to the mission of the Spirit, are in a manner of speaking 'Spiritans' and, therefore, there is a sense in which others could be called 'anonymous Spiritans' without some of the complications attached to Rahner's notion of anonymous Christians.[51]

Revelation

The second area requiring some expansion in the light of *Nostra aetate* and subsequent church documents is Revelation. There is a growing awareness among participants within inter-religious dialogue of the need for a more unified, integrated and inclusivist theology of revelation. As both *Nostra aetate* and John Paul II suggest, we must go further back beyond the biblical religions to understand the action of the Spirit of God in the world. This theology of revelation must be inclusive so that other religions may begin to recognise themselves within the discourse and language of revelation.

This means we must begin to appreciate the revelatory presence of God operative outside the mainstream of Christianity. In addition, this expanded theology of Revelation must be universal in scope, reaching back beyond the bible to the millions of people who lived before Abraham and reaching forward to touch those who, for whatever reason, live their lives removed from the major religious traditions. Lastly, this theology of revelation must move beyond those Christian fulfilment theories, which, as Aloysius Pieris points out, often 'neutralise' other religions and fail to recognise the irreducible core of other living faiths.[52]

One theologian who has provided the broad parameters of such a unified and integrated theology of revelation on the basis of the universality of God's grace in the world is Karl Rahner. Because the grace of God is 'given always and everywhere to all human beings, whether they accept it or not' there is within every human being a basic orientation and drive towards self-transcendence'.[53] It is this drive towards self-transcendence, this restless disposition within the human heart, this openness of 'spirit in matter' to the future, caused by grace, that enables the human to hear a revelation from within and without. In the light of this permanent offer of God's Self to every human being, Rahner posits a close relationship between the history of revelation and the history of the world.[54] There is in virtue of the universality of God's grace in the world what Rahner, on the one hand, calls the existence of universal Transcendental revelation (the inner word) and, on the other hand, what he refers to as the presence of particular and categorical revelation (the outer word). The whole of Rahner's theology can be read as an attempt to describe the interplay between Transcendental Revelation, available to all, and categorical revelation available in particular religious texts, traditions and rituals.

This broad, expanded and universal framework for understanding revelation must be grounded and correlated with the history of religions. Within that context Jacques Dupuis proposes that it is possible to connect and distinguish between the Monotheistic religions and the

Mystical religions of the East. The Monotheistic religions of Judaism, Christianity and Islam are made up of historical and prophetic revelation. The primary religious experience making the Monotheistic religions possible is one of 'ecstasy', some form of inter-personal encounter with God as other in history. On the other hand, the Mystical religions of the East are made up of interior moments of revelation. The primary religious experience among the Mystical religions is one of 'intasy', i.e. an interior experience 'in the cave of the heart' which entails varying elements of emptiness, absorption and unification.[55]

A Spirit-Christology

If the grace of God is universal, and if the action of the Spirit is the first self-communication of God issuing in general Revelation – and this does seem to be the teaching of the Church at Vatican II and in the post-conciliar period – then this requires the relocation of the Mystery of Christ within this wider framework. In other words, we must see Christ not only in the particular context of the originality of Judaism but also within the larger context of the universality of the action of the Spirit and the presence of grace in other religions.

How then do we relate the Christ-event to this wider history of grace? How do we connect Christ with the many responses to the universality of Spirit of God found in other religions? One way of doing this is to adopt a Spirit Christology, that is a Christology which is connected with the universal outpouring of the Spirit of God at the beginning of time as well as at the particular Pentecost recorded in the New Testament. A Spirit Christology does not mean abandoning other Christologies, such as the Logos or the Son of God or Wisdom Christologies. Instead, a Spirit Christology should be seen as complementary to these other Christologies of the New Testament. Further, a

Spirit Christology appears more suitable as a point of departure for dialogue with other religions, mainly because it has the capacity to establish some common ground and some degree of continuity between Jesus and the founders and figures of other religions.

A Spirit Christology will begin by emphasising that the Spirit of God poured out into the world at the beginning of time is the same Spirit who is now personally active and embodied in the historical life and ministry of Jesus as well as the death and destiny of Jesus. The Spirit of God enables, empowers and energises the person of Jesus throughout his life. In other words, Jesus is called, sent and filled with the Spirit of God. It is this personal presence of the Spirit of God in Jesus that others experienced when they encountered Jesus in his life, in his death and in his resurrection.

It is the Gospel of Luke that presents most consistently a Spirit Christology, with some traces also within Mark, Matthew and John. For Luke, the Spirit of God is active in the birth of Jesus by Mary (Lk 1:35). At the baptism of Jesus in the Jordan, we are told that 'the Holy Spirit descended upon him in bodily form like a dove' (Lk 3:22) and that 'Jesus, full of the Holy Spirit, returned from the Jordan and was led by the Spirit into the wilderness' (Lk 4:1) and that afterwards 'Jesus, filled with the power of the Spirit, returned to Galilee' (Lk 4:14). Further, we learn that he 'went to the synagogue on the Sabbath day, as was his custom' and 'unrolled the scroll' of Isaiah 'where it was written' (Lk 4:16, 17):

> the Spirit of the Lord is upon me,
> because he has anointed me to bring Good News to the poor ...
> release the captives,

recovery of sight to the blind, to let the oppressed go
free
to proclaim the year of the Lord's favour. (Lk 4:18-19)

Later, after the return of the seventy disciples at Pentecost,
we are told that 'Jesus rejoiced in the Holy Spirit'. We
know, in addition, it was through the power of the Spirit
that Jesus performed exorcisms and healings. Further, we
learn that Jesus offered himself up in death through the
inspiration of the Spirit and was raised to new life in the
power of the Spirit. And, finally, it was the crucified and
risen Christ who sent forth the Spirit to the community of
his disciples, described by Paul as the life-giving Spirit.

Within this expanded framework the Christ-event will
not be seen as an isolated event of the Spirit in history, nor
as some exception to the universal action of the Spirit in the
world, nor as a divine bolt of the Spirit out of the blue.
Instead we must begin to see the Christ-event as the
crystallisation of what has been going on in history through
the Spirit of God from the beginning of time, a kind of
microcosm of the action of the Spirit in the macrocosm of
life, a concentration or intensification of the Spirit's
presence in creation, a culminating point of the activity of
the Spirit in history. In brief, the Christ-event is the
historical sacrament of the Spirit of God in the world.

It is important within inter-religious dialogue to be able
to see simultaneously similarities and differences between
Christianity and other religions. In a Spirit Christology there
are some similarities between Jesus and the historical figures
of other religions: a man marked out by the Spirit of God,
mediating the Spirit of God to the world and personally
embodying the Spirit of God in a particular place and time.

It is within these similarities that Christians must affirm
significant differences between Christianity and other

religions: seeing Jesus, crucified and risen as the messiah who is the final revelation of God as Father through the power of the Spirit. In this way a Spirit Christology, when taken in conjunction with existing Christologies of the Logos, Son and Wisdom, moves towards the unfolding of a Trinitarian understanding of the one God. Further, for the Christian the shape of the Spirit of God abroad in the world and the Christian community is christomorphic, paschal and sacramental. It is christomorphic in terms of the historical life of Jesus with particular reference to the healings, exorcisms and table fellowship of the historical Jesus; it is paschal in terms of the self-emptying Spirit of God in life of Jesus that culminates in the cross; and it is sacramental in terms of particular actions that mediate the saving presence of the Spirit of God.

To sum up and conclude this reflection let me try to highlight the main points of my paper. *Nostra aetate* did effect a significant breakthrough at Vatican II and this breakthrough is best understood as a theological re-awakening, a particular awareness pointing to the action of the Spirit of God outside Christianity, the presence of the seeds of the Word in other religions, the existence of elements of truth and grace in other faiths and a ray of the truth that enlightens all. These emphases of the Council when taken together represent a significant doctrinal development and a new theological awakening. This shift is informed by a theology of the universality of the grace of God and the action of the Spirit of God in the world. This development requires an expansion of the theological imagination, with particular reference to a theology of the Spirit, revelation and Christ. Most of all, this theological shift puts Christians into a new relationship with other religions and provides a basis for new levels of dialogue and mutual enrichment. This process of dialogue and mutual enrichment has only just begun and will exercise the imagination of all religions in the coming decades. In the meantime Christians are discovering through the gift of other religions new ways of being Christian. To be Christian in the future will require among other things that we be conscious of being led by the Spirit and therefore called to be inter-religious in virtue of the action of the Spirit in other religions. In this way the Christian imagination will not only be enlarged – it will be enriched by the encounter with other religions.[56]

Notes

1. Donald Nichol, 'Other Religions (*Nostra aetate*)', *Modern Catholicism: Vatican II and After*, edited by Adrian Hastings, New York: Oxford University Press, 1991, pp. 126–127.
2. J.O. Beoszo, 'The External Climate', *History of Vatican II*, Vol. I, Giuseppe Alberigo and Joseph A. Komonchak (eds), New York: Orbis, 1995, p. 395.
3. Yves Congar, 28 September 1964, *Mon Journal du Concile,* edited and annotated by Eric Mahien, 2 Vols Paris: Cerf, 2002.
4. L. Nemer, 'Mision and Missions', *New Catholic Encyclopaedia*, second edition, Vol. 9, Washington DC: Thomson Gale in association with the Catholic University of America, 2003, p. 686.
5. F. Koenig, 'It must be the Holy Spirit', *The Tablet*, 21 December 2002, pp. 4–6 at 6.
6. 1985 Synod of Bishops, 'Final Report', Part 1, n. 5.
7. *Gaudium et spes*, n. 22.
8. *Ad gentes*, n. 4.
9. Ibid., n. 15.
10. Ibid., n. 9.
11. Ibid., n. 11.
12. Donald Nichol, 'Other Religions (*Nostra aetate*)', *Modern Catholicism:. Vatican II and After,* edited by Adrian Hastings, London: SPCK, 1991, p. 128.

13. Michael Barnes, *Theology and Dialogue*, Cambridge: CUP, 2002, p. 31
14. Mary C. Boys (ed.), 'The Enduring Covenant', *Seeing Judaism Anew: Christianity's Sacred Obligation*, New York: A Sheed and Ward Book, Rowman and Littlefield Publishers, Inc., 2005, p. 22.
15. Donald J. Moore, 'A Catholic Perspective on *NA*', in *No Religion is an Island:. The Nostra aetate Dialogue*, E. Bristow (ed.), New York: Fordham University Press, 1998, p. 13.
16. Claud Geffré, 'The Crisis of Christian Identity in an Age of Religious Pluralism' *Concilium*, 2005/3, pp. 13–26 at 17.
17. John M. Oesterreicher, 'Declaration on the Relationship of the Church to Non-Christian Religions', *Commentary on the Documents of Vatican II*, Herbert Vorgrimmler (ed.), Vol. 3, London: Burns and Oates, 1969, p. 1.
18. An indication of the vast array of such documents can be found in *Inter-Religious Dialogue: The Official Teaching of the Catholic Church (1963–1995)*, Boston: Pauline Media Books, 1997 and *John Paul II and Inter-Religious Dialogue*, B.L. Sherwin and H. Kasimow (eds), New York: Orbis, 1999.
19. See *Inter-Religious Dialogue*, edited by F. Gioia, Chapter 3, pp. 117–207.
20. *Redemptor Hominis*, a.6.
21. Ibid., n. 11.
22. *Dominum et Vivificantem*, n. 28.
23. Ibid., n. 53.
24. *Redemptoris Missio*, n. 28.
25. Ibid., n. 28–29.
26. Ibid., n. 5.
27. Ibid., n. 77.
28. Ibid., n. 55.
29. Ibid., n. 42.
30. Ibid., n. 25.
31. Ibid., n. 29.
32. The Guidelines are available in *Vatican Council: Conciliar and Post-Conciliar Documents*, A. Flannery (ed.), new revised edition, 1992, Dublin: Domincan Publications, 1992, pp. 743–749.

33. Available in *Origins*, 26 March 1998, Vol. 27, No. 40, pp. 669–674.
34. John Paul ll, address to cardinals, 22 December 1986 which is available in *Interreligious Dialogue: The Offical Teaching of the Catholic Church (1963–1995)*, F. Gioia (ed.), pp. 359–367.
35. John T. Pawlikowski, 'The Christ Event and the Jewish People', Tatha Wiley (ed.), *Thinking of Christ: Proclamation, Explanation, Meaning*, London: Continuum, 2003, pp. 103–121 at 113 and James D.G. Dunn, *The Partings of the Ways: Between Christinty and Judaism and their Significance for the Character of Christianity*, London: SCM Press, 2nd edn, 2006 (1991), especially pp. XI–XXX.
36. Michael Barnes, *Theology and the Dialogue of Religions*, Cambridge: Cambridge University Press, 2002, pp. 50, 58, 49, 54 and John Oesterreicher, 'Declaration on the Relation of the Church to Non-Christian Religions', *Commentary on the Documents of Vatican ll*, H. Vorgrimmler, Herder and Herder (eds), 1968, p. 1.
37. See Gavin D'Costa, '*Nostra aetate:* Telling God's Story in Asia: Promises and Pitfalls', *Vatican II and its Legacy*, M. Lamberigts and L. Kenis (eds), Leuven: Leuven University Press, 2002, pp. 333–334.
38. John Oesterreicher, 'Declaration on the Relation of the Church to Non-Christian Religions', *Commentary on the Documents of Vatican II*, H. Vorgrimmler, Herder and Herder (eds), 1968, pp. 90–93.
39. *LG*, a.13.
40. *LG*, a.16.
41. *Gaudium et spes*, a.25.
42. *Ad gentes*, a.9.
43. John Paul II, *Redemptoris Missio*, 7 December 1990, article 10.
44. See Dermot A. Lane, 'Rahner on Interreligious Dialogue', *Celebrating the Legacies of Karl Rahner and Bernard Lonergan: Christian Identity in a Postmodern Age*, Declan Marmion (ed.), Dublin: Veritas, 2005, pp. 91–112.
45. Karl Rahner, 'Concerning the Relationship between Nature

and Grace', *Theological Investigations*, Vol. 1, London: DLT, 1961, pp. 297–317.

46. *GS*, a.22.

47. *Redemptoris missio*, a.29.

48. See Paul Tillich, 'Significance of the History of Religions for the Systematic Theologian', *The Future of Religions*, Gerald C. Brauer (ed.), New York: Harper and Row, 1966, pp. 90–91.

49. Karl Rahner, 'Aspects of a European Theology', *Theological Investigations*, Vol. XXI, p. 97.

50. It is not my intention to replace or abandon the more traditional sequence of Father, Son and Holy Spirit. The historical sequence of Spirit, Son and Father should be seen as complementing the established theological sequence of Father, Son and Holy Spirit. A similar proposal in a different context is made by Peter Phan in 'Now that I know how to teach, What do I teach?', *Being Religious Interreligious: Asian Perspectives on Interfaith Dialogue*, New York: Orbis, 2004, pp. 38 and 38, n.65.

51. A suggestion made by Frederick Crowe in, *Son of God, Holy Spirit, and World Religions: The Contribution of Bernard Lonergan to the Wider Ecumenism*, Toront: Regus College, 1985, pp. 18. I am grateful to Ray Maloney, SJ, for bringing this item to my attention.

52. A. Pieris, *An Asian Theology of Liberation*, New York: Orbis, 1988, p. 60.

53. Paul Imhof and Hubert Biallowons (eds), *Karl Rahner in Dialogue: Conversations and Interviews 1965–1982*, New York: Crossroads, 1986, p. 750.

54. Karl Rahner, 'History of the World and Salvation History', *Theological Investigations*, Vol. 5, pp. 97–114.

55. J. Dupuis, *Christianity and the Religions: From Confrontation to Dialogue*, New York: Orbis Books, 2002, pp. 121–123.

56. I am grateful to Professor Terrence W. Tilley, Fordham University, New York, for constructive comments on an earlier version of this text.

Index

'n' following page numbers indicate a reference to a footnote and 'f' indicates a reference to a figure.

A

Abbey of Chevetonge, 191
Active participation, 86, 95, 153
Ad gentes (Decree on the Mission Activity of the Church), 208, 224
Adult religious education, 167, 182
Advent, 33, 34
Age, for ordination to the priesthood, 17
Alive-O, 173, 175–176
Anonymous Christianity, 40
Apostolic Tradition of Hippolytus, 90
Apostolos Suos (apostolic letter), 61
Assemblies, 62
Assisi, gathering of all religions at, 216–217

B

Baptism, 194
Baptism, Eucharist and Ministry, 64
Barth, Karl, 50
Bea, Cardinal, 16, 24, 203, 204
Beauduin, Lambert, 86–87, 88

Benedict XVI, Pope, 32, 50, 52, 63, 71, 116
on communion ecclesiology, 66
on *Dei verbum*, 101
Erasmus lecture (1988), 111
on *Gaudium et spes*, 33–34
on God is Love, 53
inaugural address (extract), 41
on Vatican II, 10–11, 51
Benedictine monasteries, 84
Bible, the, 96
divine authorship, 114–115
historical-critical analysis of, 112–113
meaning of, 114–117
'The Interpretation of the Bible in the Church', 100–101, 110, 111, 116
use in the Liturgy, 118
Bible history classes, 150
Bidding prayers (prayer of the faithful), 96
Bishops
Decree on the Pastoral Office of Bishops, 155
and religious education, 156
Brown, Raymond, 111

Browne, Michael (Cardinal), 24
Buchberger, Bishop, 50–51
Buddhism, 206
Bulgakov, Sergius, 62
Byrne, Gareth, 181

C
Casel, Odo, 90
Catechesi tradendae, 168, 169
Catechesis, 164
   and evangelisation, 169
Catechetical Association of Ireland, 166
Catechism, 148–149
Catechism of the Catholic Church, 148, 171–172
Categorical revelation, 228
Catholic Principles of Ecumenism, 188
Catholicity, 62
Catholics
   and ecumenism before Vatican II, 189–191
   relationship between Jews and, 203
Central Preparatory Committee, 16–17
Charles, Peter, 17
Children
   Eucharistic Prayers for Masses with Children, 154
   introducing image of God in *Alive-O*, 175
   involvement in celebration of the Mass, 153–154
   The Directory for Masses with Children, 153
Children of God series, 165, 170, 173
Christian Religious Education, Tom Groome, 163
Christian Way series, 162, 170
Christian worship, 90
Christianity, Jewishness of, 218

Christians
   Jews and, 141
   rifts between, 188
Church Dogmatics, Karl Barth, 50
Church, the
   charismatic profile of, 69
   decree on the mission activity of (*Ad gentes*), 208, 224
   Dogmatic Constitution on the Church (*Lumen gentium*), 25, 33, 52, 69, 70, 152, 153, 207
   in the Modern World, Pastoral Constitution on, *see Gaudium et spes*
Church music, 86
Churches and Ecclesial Communities Separated from the Roman Apostolic See, 193
Commission for Relations with the Jews, 215
Communion, 53, 55–57, 195
   Pope John Paul II on, 56–57
   spirituality of, 67–68
Community of Faith, 180
Community of Hope, 180
Community of Love, 180
Compendium of the Social Doctrine of the Church, 43, 46–48
Conciliarity, 58, 61–63
Confalonieri, Cardinal, 18
Confirmation, 168
Congar, Yves, 25, 28, 29, 199
   on anti-semitism, 205
   on Archbishop Wojtyla, 25
   Divided Christendom, 191
Congregation for Rites of the Curia, 95
Constitution on the Church in the Modern World, *see Gaudium et spes*
Constitution on the Sacred Liturgy (*Sacrosanctum concilium*), 81–98, 152, 153
Conway, Cardinal, 20, 159–160

Council of Chalcedon, 59
'Council Digest', 21
Council of Ephesus, 59
Council Hall, 19
Council of Nicea, 59
Council of Trent, 189
Councils, 58
    examples of, 59
    involving lay people, 60
Creation, 43
Cule, Bishop, 26
Cullman, Oscar, 195

D
Dalton, Cardinal, 20
Daly, Cahal (Bishop)
    foreword to *Christian Way*
    series (extract), 162
    on post primary religious
    education in 1960s, 156–158
De fontibus revelationis, 99, 130
De Lubac, Henri, 28
    on the Word of God, 133
De Smedt, Bishop, 24, 120n
Declaration on the Church's
    relation to Non-Christian
    Religions, *see Nostra aetate*
Decree on Ecumenism, *see*
    Restoration of Unity among
    Christians
Decree on the Pastoral Office of
    Bishops, 155
Decretum de Iudaeis, 204
Deenihan, Tom, on religion as an
    examination subject, 179
Dei verbum (Document on Divine
    Revelation), 52, 152
    actualisation problem, 118–120
    brief analysis of, 101–106
    chapter 4
        Article 14, 137–138
        Article 15, 138–139, 140–141
        Article 16, 140–141

commentary by A. Grillmeier,
    106
critical observations, 106–109
depiction of God's plan
    (*oeconomia salutis*), 107
on exegetes, 106
God's revelation to humankind,
    154
historicity and *Sachkritik*
    problem, 117–118
meaning of the sacred text,
    114–117
on the Old Testament, 116
relation between Scripture and
    Tradition, 102–104
relationship between the Old
    Testament and the New
    Testament, 136–145
relevance of, 109
Sacred Scripture, 105–106
use of the Bible in the Liturgy,
    118
Vatican II and, 99–100
see also divine revelation
Dialogue
    of action, 213
    inter-religious, 213
    of life, 213
    of religious experience, 214
    of theological exchange,
    213–214
Dialogue and Proclamation:
    Reflections and Orientations on
    Inter-Religious Dialogue and
    the Proclamation of the Gospel
    of Jesus Christ, 212–214
Dibelius, Otto, 50
Didache, the, 90
Directory for Children's Masses,
    The, 153
Divided Christendom, Yves Congar,
    191
Divine Afflante Spirito, 93
Divine revelation, 130–135, 154

see also Dei verbum (Document on Divine Revelation)

Divine self-communication, 131

Do this in Memory of Me, Maeve Mahon and Martin Delaney, 186n

Dogmatic Constitution on the Church (*Lumen gentium*), 25, 33, 52, 69, 70, 152, 153, 207

Dominum et Vivificantem (encyclical), 67, 212

Dominus Iesus, 214–215

Dupuis, Jacques, 229

E

Earth, the, resources of, 43

Eastern Orthodox churches, 188

Ecclesiae sanctae, 60

Ecclesial communities, 71, 193

Ecclesiam Suam (encyclical), 211

Ecclesiology, 196–199

Ecumenism, 61, 187–201
    advances in, 194–196
    Catholic principles of, 188
    ecumenical guidelines, 24
    Vatican II and, 191–194

Education Act (1998), 178

Egeria, the diary of, 90

Elliott, Charles, *Locating the Energy for Change*, 174

Episcopal conferences, 60, 61

Eucharistic liturgy, 96

Eucharistic Prayers for Masses with Children, 154

Evangeli nuntiandi, 168, 169

Evangelisation, 168
    catechesis and, 169

Exegetes, 106

Experience of God: An Invitation to do Theology, The, Dermot Lane, 163

Extraordinary Synod of Bishops (1985), guidelines for interpretation of the Second Vatican Council, 9–10, 207

F

Faith, 154, 169, 195

Faith Friend Programme for Confirmation, 168

Faith and Order Conference (1927), 189

Faith and Order Louvain Report (1971), 62–63

Faith Seeking Understanding, 180–181

Fameree, Joseph, *Legitimate Diversity in the Roman Catholic Tradition*, 197

Family, the, 42, 169

Feeney, Leonard, 190

Felici, Archbishop, 19, 27

Fidei Depositum (Apostolic Constitution), views on *Catechism of the Catholic Church*, 171–172

First Vatican Council, end of, 15

Frings, Cardinal, 23, 50, 51

G

Gaudium et spes (Pastoral Constitution on the Church in the Modern World), 25, 31–48, 152, 208, 224, 225
    anthropology of, 39, 40
    change in society since publication of, 36–37
    destiny of the earth's resources, 43
    during Advent, 33
    encouragement of dialogue, 155
    evaluation of, 34–39
    on international community, 45–46
    theological anthropology, 40

use of language of dialogue, 32
  on war, 44–45
General Catechetical Directory,
  155, 172
General Directory for Catechesis,
  170, 172, 175
*Gift of Authority: Authority in the
  Church III, The*, 64
Globalisation, 43, 220
God
God's grace as the key to inter-
  religious dialogues, 222–224
  introducing image of God in
  Alive-O, 175
  salvation of, 207–208
  Vatican II on, 52–56
God and Man series, 161
Gospel, proclamation of the, 213
Gospel of Luke, Spirit Christology,
  230
Gospels, authors of the, 108
Grace, 222–224
  Nature and, 222–223
Greville, Brid, Sr, 162
Groome, Tom, *Christian Religious
  Education*, 163
Group des Dombes, 65
Guardini, Romano, 50
Guéranger, Prosper, 84

H
Handing On Faith In The Home,
  169
Hemmerle, Klaus, on the Trinity, 131
Hinduism, 206
Historical-critical method, of
  scriptural interpretation, 125,
  126, 134
Holy Spirit, Pope John Paul II on,
  67
Holy Trinity, 131
Humani Generis (False Trends in
  Modern Teaching) (encyclical), 28

I
Institutes, for training religious
  educators, 158–159
Inter-religious dialogue, 213
  God's grace as the key to,
  222–224
International community, 45–46
'Interpretation of the Bible in the
  Church', 100–101, 110, 111,
  115–116
Into the Classroom series, 180
Ireland
  in the 1960s, 151–152
  in the 1990s, 173–174
Irish Biblical Association, 119
Irish Bishops' Conference,
  catechetical methodologies, 156
Isaac, Jules, 203
*Islands Apart: A Report on the
  Children of God Series*, Martin
  Kennedy, 182–183

J
Jesus, as doorway to the Upper
  Room of the Church, 72–74
*Jewish People and their Sacred
  Scriptures in the Christian
  Bible, The*, Pontifical Biblical
  Commission, 141–142
*Jewish People and their Sacred
  Scriptures in Christianity, The*,
  216
Jews
  Commission for Relations with
  the Jews, 215
  relationship between Catholics
  and, 203
  relationship between Christians
  and, 141
John Paul II, Pope, 25, 29
  on the Church and art, 183
  on communion, 56–57, 67–68
  Dominum et Vivificantem
  (encyclical), 67, 212

on economic activity, 42
on ecumenism in *Ut Unum Sint*, 61
on Laity, 57
Novo millennio Ineunte, 56
prophetic gestures by, 216–218
Redemptor Hominis (encyclical), 212
Redemptoris Missio (encyclical), 212, 225
on salvation in Christ, 224
'The Interpretation of the Bible in the Church', 100–101
universal catechism, 171
John XXIII, Pope, 14, 18, 19, 20, 21
death of, 29–30
homily on opening day of Second Vatican Council, 22–23
opening speech, 67
relationship of Catholics and Jews, 203
Joseph, St, 26
Judaism, 206, 217, 218

K
Kasper, Walter, 52, 65
on mystery of communion, 55
on 'People of God' images, 54–55
Kehl, Medhard, 70
Kennedy, Martin, *Islands Apart: A Report on the Children of God Series*, 182–183
Kennelly, Brendan, methodology of religious education, 149
Kerrigan, Alexander, 24
Kerygmatic approach, 150, 151
Koinonia, 195, 198

L
La Nouvelle Theologie, 222
Lane, Dermot
on social justice, 171

The Experience of God: An Invitation to do Theology, 163
Law of mutual love, 72–73
Lay Christians, 48
Legitimate Diversity in the Roman Catholic Tradition, Joseph Fameree, 197
Lexikon für Theologie und Kirche, 51
Lienart, Cardinal, 23
Liturgical Institutes, 94
Liturgical Movement, 82, 83–93
Liturgical renewal, projects, 88–92
Liturgy
Constitution on the Sacred (*Sacrosanctum concilium*), 81–98, 152, 153
reforms prior to Vatican II, 94
study weeks, 91–92
Liturgy the Life of the Church, 87
Liturgy scholars, 89
Locating the Energy for Change, Charles Elliott, 174
Long, Seán, on religion as Leaving Certificate subject, 176
Looney, Anne, on teaching religion in post primary schools, 176–177
Lumen gentium (Dogmatic Constitution on the Church), 25, 33, 52, 69, 70, 152, 153, 207

M
McGahern, John, extract from *Memoir*, 146–147
McKenna, Bobby, 159
McQuaid, John Charles, 9, 20
Marriage, 42
Mater Dei Institute of Education, 9, 158–159
Maynooth Catechism, The, 149
Mediator Dei (encyclical), 93
Message to the People of God, 168

Michel, Virgil, 88, 89
Missionary activity, decree on the
   Church's (*Ad gentes*), 208, 224
Missions, encyclical on the
   (*Redemptoris Missio*), 212
Mixed marriages, 194
Monastery printing presses, 85
Monotheistic religions, 229
Montini, Cardinal, *see* Paul VI,
   Pope
Motu proprio, 60
Mount Oliver Institute of Religious
   Education, 159
Multiculturalism, 219–220
Murphy-O'Connor, Cormac
   (Cardinal), 195
Muslims, 206
The Mystical Body of Christ, 190
Mystical religions, of the East, 229
Mystici Corporis (encyclical), 93

N
Nature, and Grace, 222–223
Nature and Purpose of the Church,
   64
New Testament
   allusions and quotations in *Dei
      verbum*, 138f
   images describing the Church,
      54
   relationship between Old
      Testament and, 136–145
Nichol, Donald, 209
Non-Christian Religions,
   Declaration on the Church's
   Relation to, *see Nostra aetate*
Nostra aetate, 52, 202–236
   article 1, 205
   article 2, 205–206
   article 3, 206
   article 4, 206–207
   article 5, 207
   background to, 203–205
   breakthroughs at Vatican II, 232

challenges arising from,
   218–233
evaluation of, 209–211
reception in the post-conciliar
   period, 211–216
relation to other documents at
   Vatican II, 207–209
summary of, 205–207
*Notes on the Correct Way to
   Present Jews and Judaism in
   Preaching and Catechesis in the
   Roman Catholic Church*, 215

O
Oesterreicher, John, 223
O'Hare, Breige, 168
Old Testament
   allusions and quotations in *Dei
      verbum*, 138f
   Dei verbum (Document on
      divine revelation) on the, 116
   purpose of, 138–139
   references in *Dei verbum*,
      137–138
   relationship between New
      Testament and, 136–145
'On the Attitude of Catholics
   Toward Non-Christians and
   especially toward Jews', 204
'On the Jews and Non-Christians',
   205
On Our Way series, 151
O'Neill, Donal, on religion as
   examination subject, 177
O'Neill, Una, on religious
   education, 183
Opening day, Second Vatican
   Council, 22
Orate Fratres (now *Worship*), 89
Ordination to the priesthood, age
   for, 17
Orthodox churches, 193
Ottaviani, Cardinal, 16

P

Parente, Archbishop, 27
Pastor Aeternus, 49
Pastoral Constitution on the
    Church in the Modern World,
    see Gaudium et spes
Pastoral experimentation, 92
Paul VI, Pope, 23, 24, 27, 30, 168
    Ecclesiam Suam (encyclical), 211
Peace movements, 45
Pentecost, 67
'People of God', image of the
    Church, 54
Philbin, Bishop, 20, 25
Philips, Gerard, 28, 29
Pieris, Aloysius, 228
Piolanti, Mgr, 27
Pius X, Pope, on active
    participation of the people in
    the liturgy, 86
Pius XI, Pope
    on ecumenical movement, 190
    proposal to reconvene Vatican
    I, 15–16
Pius XII, Pope, 16, 190
    Humani Generis (encyclical), 28
Pneumatology, 226
Pontifical Biblical Commission, *The
    Jewish People and their Sacred
    Scriptures in the Christian
    Bible*, 141–142
Poor, the, 43
Post-Shoah theology, 218
Poverty, 42
Prayers of the faithful, 96
Pre-Chalcedonian churches, 188, 193
Preparation, for Vatican II, 19
Priesthood, age for ordination to
    the, 17
Primary School Curriculum (1971),
    165–166
Protestant Reformation, 188
Publishing, of missals, 89

Q

*Questions Liturgiques/Studies in
    Liturgy*, 87, 89

R

Rahner, Karl, 28, 226, 228
    on God's grace, 224
    on spirituality of the Church, 68
Ratzinger, Joseph, *see* Benedict
    XVI, Pope
Redemptor Hominis (encyclical),
    212
Redemptoris Missio (encyclical),
    212, 225
Religion
    in contemporary society, 218–219
    in the home, 169–170
    spirit-centred theology of,
    225–227
    as subject in Leaving
    Certificate, 176–180
Religion teachers, 158
Religion Teachers Associations, 166
Religious education, 9, 146–186
    adult, 167
    before Vatican II, 146–151
    catechetical materials, 160
    catechetical methodologies, 164
    enrichment by the arts, 183
    in post primary schools, 156,
    176, 178
    syllabus for primary schools,
    164, 181
Religious Liberty, debate on, 27–28
Religious practice, in Western
    societies, drop in, 41
Renehan, Caroline, 180
Research, into ancient liturgical
    texts, 89–91
*Restoration of Unity among
    Christians* (*Unitatis
    redintegratio*), 187
    Catholic Principles of
    Ecumenism, 188

chapter 2, 191–192
chapter 3, 193
introduction, 187
Revelation, 103, 227–229
Rite of Christian Initiation of
    Adults, 167
Robinson, Mary, 173, 175
Rogan, Edward, on use of the
    catechism, 148
Romanticism, 83
Roncalli, Angelo Giuseppe, *see*
    John XXIII, Pope
Ruffini, Cardinal, 26

S
Sacred Liturgy, Constitution on the,
    see Sacrosanctum concilium
Sacred tradition, 134
Sacrosanctum concilium
    (Constitution on the Sacred
    Liturgy), 81–98, 152
    achievements of, 95–97
    active participation in the
    liturgy, 153
Salvation, 108, 195
Schmemann, Alexander, 62
Scripture, 96, 109–120
    and Tradition, 23–24, 102–104,
    133–134
Second Vatican Council, *see* Vatican
    II
Secularisation, 41
Self-transcendence, 228
Seminaries, liturgy courses in, 91
Situation of Catechesis in Ireland,
    182
Slipyj, Archbishop, 27
Sobernost, 62
Social justice, 171
Social teaching, in the Church, 47
Spirit, the, 70, 225
    role of, 212
Spirit-centred theology, of religions,
    225–227

Spirit-Christology, 229–233
Spiritual sense, definition, 115
Study weeks, 91–92
Suenens, Cardinal, 24
Sunday worship, 95
Synod of Bishops, 35, 60
Synods, 58–61
    and the Church's Upper Room,
    65–71

T
Tardini, Cardinal, 18
Textbooks, for Junior cycle religion
    students, 180
Theological imagination, 221
Tijdschrift voor Liturgie, 89
Tillard, Jean Marie, 196
Tillich, Paul, 225
Tra le sollecitudini (apostolic letter),
    86, 87
Tradition, and Scripture, 102–105,
    133–134
Traditions, 122n
Transcendental Revelation, 228
Trinity, the, 131

U
Ultramontanist movement, 84
*Un seul Maître: L'autorité
    Doctrinale dans l'Eglise*, 64
Unitatis redintegratio (The
    Restoration of Unity among
    Christians), 187
'Upper Room', of the Church, 66,
    72–74
Ut Unum Sint (May they all be
    One), 61

Vacchini, Francesco, 19
Vatican I, end of, 15
Vatican II
    constitutions of, 11
    ecumenism and, 191–194
    Irish contribution to, 20

key days, 22–28
proceedings commentaries, 29
secrecy of, 20
and synodality, 58–61
Vernacular language, 97
Vernacular missals, 85–86

W
War, 44–45
Wardi, Chain, 204
We Remember: A Reflection on the Shoah, 215

Willebrands, Cardinal, 197
Williams, Kevin, on religion as an examination subject, 179–180
Williamson, Peter S., 115
Wojtyla, Karol, *see* John Paul II, Pope
Word of God, 132–133
World Council of Churches, 61, 62
World Day of Peace, 32
Worship (formerly *Orate Fratres*), 89